# LEARNING COMMUNITIES AND IMAGINED SOCIAL CAPITAL

Also available from Continuum

*Education and Community,* Dianne Gereluk

*Transforming Learning in Schools and Communities,*
Bob Lingard, Jon Nixon and Stewart Ranson

# Learning Communities and Imagined Social Capital

*Learning to Belong*

Jocey Quinn

Continuum Studies in Educational Research

continuum

**Continuum International Publishing Group**

The Tower Building　　　　　80 Maiden Lane
11 York Road　　　　　　　　Suite 704
London SE1 7NX　　　　　　　New York NY 10038

www.continuumbooks.com

First published 2010
Paperback edition first published 2011

**British Library Cataloguing-in-Publication Data**
A catalogue record for this book is available from the British Library.

ISBN: 9781847061928 (hardback)
ISBN: 9781441124203 (paperback)

**Library of Congress Cataloging-in-Publication Data**
Quinn, Jocey.
Learning communities and imagined social capital : learning to belong /
Jocey Quinn.
　　　p. cm. — (Continuum studies in educational research)
　　Includes bibliographical references.
　　ISBN 978-1-4411-2420-3 (pbk.) – ISBN 978-1-84706-192-8 (hbk.) – ISBN
978-1-4411-3906-1 (ebk.) 1. Adult education—Great Britain. 2. Continuing
education—Great Britain. 3. Social capital (Sociology) I. Title. II. Series.

　　LC5256.G7Q56 2011
　　374'.941–dc23
　　　　　　　　　　　　　2011025087

Typeset by Pindar NZ, Auckland, New Zealand
Printed and bound in Great Britain

# Contents

# Introduction

*Decided to write a notebook as part of the book project – want to use it as a thread throughout – process of writing and learning and tracing spaces, symbolic connections vs. enforced communities, generative moments vs. legislated 'learning outcomes' . . . Sitting upstairs in the bedroom by the window watching the tide come in and some geese overhead, what a joy and so lucky. Resolved to treasure the moments and the days and make this book part of a creative time.*

*(J. Q., research diary)*

This book is a culmination of thinking about and researching adults learning in many different contexts: in universities, at work, in voluntary sector projects and informally. With my notebook as a thread I have enjoyed writing it, although the time of writing has been one of difficulty as well as creativity. Throughout my research I have thought long and hard about what role learning plays in the process of belonging. Belonging is not a solid formation, it is:

> . . . the desire for some sort of attachment, be it to other people, places or modes of being . . . wanting to belong, wanting to become, a process that is fuelled by yearning rather than the positioning of identity as a stable state.

(Probyn 1996, p. 21)

In these terms, belonging is not a conservative matter which inexorably fixes the subject, but an endless process: 'the inbetweenness of belonging, of belonging not in some deep authentic way but belonging in constant movement, modes of belonging as surface shifts' (ibid., p. 21). Such a fluid vision has led me to critique the notion of 'learning community', since learn-ing communities act as regulated tools for a belonging which is forged of limits, not possibilities. Instead, I argue that what I have termed 'imagined social capital' plays a far more important and creative role in the lives of learners, in responding to and fostering their yearning to belong. In this book I am seeking to bring these opposed elements of learning community and imagined social capital together and to take the opportunity to think more deeply and discursively about these issues. From my perspective this is a luxurious opportunity. I hope it is also a timely intervention, when the concept of learning community is so pervasive across the educational landscape, and yet so unproblematized, and when the significance of the imagined and symbolic in learners' lives is neglected. The aims of the book are twofold: one is to develop generative and innovative thinking about learning, in a spirit of pleasure, the other is to pay critical attention to the needs of learners and to make a material difference in this world. These aims are not antithetical but interdependent.

## Introduction to textual and theoretical approach

As an introduction to the book I would like to explain some of my modes of working. This will be a hybrid text which employs Dorothy E. Smith's (1999) fertile idea of using multiple and indirectly related readings as 'proxies to the text'; finding in other sources, such as literature, poetry and my own research diaries, moments of illumination or expansion of ideas which I then bring to the discussion. Smith described how, while she was researching or writing about a sociological issue, other readings, which were appar-ently unconnected, and which she was reading for pleasure, or in other contexts, gave her insights which helped her to unravel and understand the sociological problem. I have also found this to be true in my own work. The concept perhaps only makes explicit what happens in all texts, for, as de Certeau argues: 'Every particular study is a multi-faceted mirror (others reappear everywhere in this space) reflecting the exchanges, readings and confrontations that form the conditions of its possibility' (de Certeau 1984,

p. 44). This multiplicity of textual sources mirrors the diversity of research accounts on which I will be drawing and the range of theoretical perspectives that I shall employ to analyze them, taken primarily from educational research, feminist theory, human geography and cultural studies. It is important that this book is both strongly theoretical and deeply grounded in empirical studies, and that the mutual relationship between these two factors is absolutely integral.

The necessity and role of theory within educational research and the humanities and social sciences generally has become a hot topic (Thomas 2007). As Auden did of poetry, Thomas argues that theory 'makes nothing happen' and that it has become both reified and used to camouflage the bankruptcy of academic studies in making or predicting change. In the education field at least, it does seem rather premature to discard theory when so much educational writing consists of un-analytical and highly descriptive accounts of practice. Similarly it is disingenuous to refuse or refute theory when theorizing is a key part of everyday life. We are always theorizing or turning to theory, creating or adopting explanations for what is happening to us and why we do the things we do. Some theories are more sophisticated and illuminating than others, but theory making is unavoidable. From my perspective, the everyday nature of theory links to the significance of everyday empirical data:

> . . . yes the sharing of these moments. I'm constantly looking at different ways of taking or highlighting moments like these which I have all the time. I find my daily life a very exciting arena; the small actions, tastes, sights, observations, discoveries that are so thrilling.
>
> (Performance artist Bobby Baker, quoted in Heathfield 2007, p. 85)

Thrilling indeed to enter this everyday arena and use it to highlight theoretical understandings, yet relationships between theoretical and empirical imperatives seem increasingly fractious. I have recently encountered interesting discussions about the necessity of empirical data in the generation of theory. Gert Biesta has made distinctions between 'autonomous theorising' and empirical research (Biesta 2009), while participants at the international

Gender and Education Conference (Institute of Education, London, April 2009) argued whether sociology could be practiced without empirical data and came to no agreed conclusion. While conceding that abstract theorizing is a possibility, and indeed more useful than data untroubled by theory (the depressing feature of much educational writing), the most powerful theorizing is generated by attempts to resolve problems and paradoxes thrown up by empirical study, rather than trying to predict the future. Moreover, as Beverley Skeggs has powerfully argued (Skeggs 1997), research participants are often much more adept and evocative in conceptualizing their own lives than we as researchers are. In my experience, the very words and images that they use may generate new theoretical understandings. The appropriations and resistances practised by people in everyday life often confound the value assumptions of researchers. This leaves polemical statements about what is good or bad for others as rather empty and indefensible. Thus, my position in this book is that theory does matter in framing and pushing new understandings and visions, but whatever theorizing I am doing here is emerging through and from the empirical, rather than being imposed upon it.

## Introduction to the research studies

So who are the people I will be learning from in this book? The book will draw on qualitative data from over 200 learners, taken from four different research studies. First I will explore data from the higher education (HE) sector. This includes my Economic and Social Research Council funded doctoral research, which was an in-depth study involving 21 diverse women students, including both working class and middle class women, aged from 19 to 62, in their second year of interdisciplinary degrees in post-1992 universities in the UK (Quinn 2003a). The purpose of the research was to analyze how far the mass participation of women and the growth of feminist ideas had impacted on the curriculum and culture of universities, and how the studying experience was interacting with their lives outside the university, in shaping the subjectivities of these women students. The universities were higher education institutions, with comparatively recent or newly negotiated university status, located in the same city, who both prioritized widening participation and might be anticipated to be open to cultural change. In the research they are given the pseudonyms Expanding University and Pleasant College. American Studies and Environmental Studies were chosen as disciplines which could provide a broad and interdisciplinary mix where curricular change might seem most likely. This research involved a range of qualitative methods. I began by conducting focus groups across the four courses. Here I used prompts such as a video about eco-feminism and a video of the American author Toni Morrison to stimulate discussion about feminist ideas and how far they had influenced the curriculum studied by these students. The focus groups also discussed how far feminist ideas coupled with the mass participation of women students were influencing pedagogical practices and the culture of the university generally. At a later date this was followed by in-depth interviews where participants explored their own life histories, how they had been constructed as women within them and the role that university education was playing in their subjectivities. They also addressed their experiences of and attitudes towards feminism. Subsequently a number of the students kept week-long participant diaries. Here they were given prompts to reflect at length on the daily process of their studies and the events in their daily lives, in order to explore how these factors interacted and the ways in which the curriculum positioned them as subjects. The diaries provoked many issues such as bodies and disability, sexuality, male violence, ageing, whiteness, motherhood and relationships with mothers. As well as the rich data generated by these interactions with women students, I also observed seminars and lectures, analysed curricular materials and key documents such as Mission statements and conducted a loose ethnography of the different institutional spaces.

The second higher education-based study on which I am drawing was conducted for the Joseph Rowntree Foundation as part of their 'Ladders out of Poverty Programme' (see Quinn *et al.* 2005). This study sought to explore the meanings and implications of the high rates of 'dropout' from university amongst working class students. The central question that we sought to address was: if higher education is traditionally seen as a ladder out of poverty, why were these students climbing down the ladder and jumping off, even when they had few alternative job prospects and were studying in institutions which were designed to welcome and support them? We were also interested in the interaction of student dropout and local cultures and the potential impacts on poverty and decline in these areas. The study was based in four provincial areas across the UK in England, Wales, Scotland and Northern Ireland that had experienced declining traditional industries such as pottery and mining. The students had dropped out of universities that prioritized widening participation and which were taking a role in local regeneration. It included interviews with 67 first generation students aged under 25 who had dropped out of university, 40 of whom were men, all but one of whom were white and working class.

The project was a qualitative, participative study which began with a method that we termed research jury days, held in the four locations and involving a total of 120 stakeholders. The purpose of these days was to bring together a wide range of participants including students, lecturers, support staff, employers, employment agencies and representatives from the voluntary sector to explore dropout from multiple perspectives. The events involved invited presentations and discussions, analyzing dropout and its impacts on the locality, presented to a jury of researchers. This resulted in a contextualized and localized understanding of the issue, which reconceptualized dropout as a socio-cultural phenomenon, rather than the individual problem of student or university (see Quinn 2004a, for a full discussion). The jury days were followed by in-depth interviews with the 67 students who had withdrawn early, an international colloquium and policy seminar, interviews with Careers and Employment agencies and an Admissions survey. The study allowed us to explore some of the meanings and implications of dropout and to theorize and rethink the issue. Along with the student interviews, I will also be employing data from other stakeholders involved in the study, such as lecturers, support staff and other local agencies.

Moving into the sphere of more informal learning, I will be drawing on a research project on 'learning brokerage': the ways in which relationships are mediated between 'hard-to-reach learners' and formal educational institutions (Thomas *et al.* 2004). In this project we saw learning as a chain involving many different people and services. My role in this study, which was funded by the Learning and Skills Research Centre, included leading case studies conducted with voluntary sector organizations which ran different forms of learning activities (see Quinn *et al.* 2004). It is these case studies that I am employing here. The case studies involved interviews and discussions with learners themselves, plus interviews with project staff, observations, and meetings with partner organizations. The focus of the study was to explore how learning took place in these non-traditional spaces, the role that learning played in the lives of learners who were relatively marginalized and disadvantaged and the ways in which links were being made across to the formal educational system and other agencies. The first study involved interviews and focus groups with five homeless adults, who were aged between 25 and 35, primarily white, male and working class and who were engaged in informal learning activities in a learning centre attached to a homeless charity in a large city in England. The second featured interviews and focus groups with 20 young people between the ages of 16 and 25, mainly black, male and working class, who were involved in two community arts projects in inner city areas of London. I will be using data from these interviews and from interviews and focus groups held with staff from the projects and linked organizations.

Finally, I will be analysing interview data from a study of 114 young adults aged 16–19 from rural areas of south-west England, who are classed as being in 'jobs without training' (JWT). These are young people who are all around us, but tend to be invisible. They do jobs that do not have access to accredited training, such as working in shops, hotels and on building sites and farms, and they have left school without what is considered the target level of qualifications in the UK, which is five GCSEs graded A to C. Being 'a young person in JWT' is essentially a policy construct and has been defined as being employed for more than 16 hours per week, but not engaged in any form of formal training leading to nationally recognized qualifications at Level 2 or above and not having qualifications at Level 2. Thus those classified as 'young people in jobs without training' are defined entirely in terms of lack: their jobs lack such accredited training and they themselves are deemed to be lacking in prospects. The policy push is to provide this group of young people with training and educational opportunities to enhance and develop their skills so that they can compete more effectively in the job market. This policy-driven conceptualization of JWT provided the frame for our research, because it is this group of young people who have been identified as in need of intervention. While young people in JWT are not placed at the bottom of the hierarchy of social and economic concern, like those who are categorized as NEET (not in education, employment or training), they are perceived as having low levels of functional literacy and numeracy, combined with a deficit of life and vocational skills. They are often treated as if they too have no employment and the work that they do is devalued and ignored. Such young people are commonly characterized as 'dead-end kids in dead-end jobs', yet very little is actually known about their lives, their work and their priorities.

These young people, roughly equal numbers of males and females, were mostly working class and all but one were white. They are not in formal education but are still learning, either in the workplace or in informal settings. The purpose of the study (Quinn *et al.* 2008), was to explore their experiences and perceptions of work and learning. This study was co-funded by the European Social Fund, Connexions and the Learning and Skills Council. There were three strands of research methods in this project: qualitative research with these young people, participatory research with stakeholders such as local authorities, employers and youth workers and capacity building research with personal advisers from Connexions, who was the agency given the role to provide careers advice and guidance to such young people. The young people were interviewed either face-to-face by the project researcher or by telephone by Connexions advisers, or took part in a small focus group led by the research team. The research data comprises 182 interviews with young people aged 16–21, 155 by telephone and 27 face-to-face, plus a focus group with three young people. A total of 114 were interviewed once and 68 of these were re-interviewed at least four months later, 13 face-to-face and the rest by telephone. The sample was selected by Connexions, who was able to ensure from its records that these young people did not have Level 2 qualifications and were not engaged in Level 2 training at the start of the research. As well as data from the interviews I will also be referring to research diaries kept by some personal advisers as part of the project.

From the accounts above, it is clear that this book is unusual in involving a very diverse group of learners, ranging in age from 16 to 62. They come from across the UK: England, Wales, Scotland and Northern Ireland and from different types of settings: urban, metropolitan, provincial and rural. These people are disparate, as are the learning activities they are involved in, which move across the continuum of formal and informal activities. They are not elite learners, but are generally placed in a problematic and marginal position to the formal education system. The studies which involved them had different purposes, but they all have a unifying interest in the relationships between cultural shifts, knowledge transformations and social justice. For example, they explored how the mass participation of women impacted on the culture and curriculum of universities; the relationships between working class dropout from universities and localized social inequality and how marginalized groups such as homeless adults and those young people perceived as just 'dead-end kids in dead-end jobs' understood the role of learning in their lives. Despite their marginalization, all these participants were engaged in generating forms of imagined social capital. They are not victims or problems, but complex figures who can help unravel the processes of learning to belong.

Although the participants in this book are all from the UK, it is important to place them within global maps of belonging. Their lives are part of a web of connections across the world. It is easy to unpick some strands of the web. Some of the homeless people had experienced heroin addiction and so were linked to a global market of drug production, movement and policing. The young black men in the arts organizations were involved in learning and playing rap music, making explicit connections with black urban experience in the USA. The students who lived in areas of declining traditional industry and had dropped out of university in their local area are the products of worldwide shifts in production. Their lives have to be understood as being formed by these shifts and trends as well as contributing to them:

It's a deprived area round here. It's below the EU-stated poverty line. Without students going to university I don't think it's going to be able to get out of that. It's a catch-22 situation: you need the students to go to university in order to increase the economic standing of the area. Not many big businesses want to come to an area where the population isn't educated . . . like I say it goes round and round.

(education officer, Students Union, research jury day)

For the young people in the south-west, their working lives are influenced by patterns of migration from Europe, as they work alongside or compete for low-paid jobs with workers from Eastern Europe. In contrast, the women studying in university are the privileged beneficiaries of global feminist movements and the massive cultural shift towards the mass participation of women in higher education in the West.

None of these lines of connection are innocent ones; they are produced by global movements of capitalism and imperial legacies. As Alexander argues, no one is exempt from the consequences of the colonial past which echo through our daily lives, for 'we are living witnesses or casualties of empire's egregious practices' (Alexander 2005, p. 2). In exploring their relationships to learning I am also interrogating these connections and entering into a global picture which has resonance beyond the confines of the UK. This does not mean that these learners are the passive recipients of such global movements or that they are without agency. As de Certeau points out, practices of resistance and subversion accompany such movements. For example, indigenous Indians colonized by the Spanish:

> often used the laws, practices and representation that were imposed on them . . . to ends other than those of their conquerors; they made something else out of them . . . They metaphorized the dominant order: they made it function in another register. They remained other within the system which they assimilated and which assimilated them externally. They diverted it without leaving it.
>
> (de Certeau, op. cit., p. 32)

So too for the learners in these studies. They cannot escape the system, but diversion is always a possibility. The balance maintained between the 'diversions' they are able to make and their assimilation by systems of domination is one of the issues I shall explore in this book.

In bringing this data together, I am aware of the pitfalls of neglecting the differentials between participants and of the effect of various methodological approaches and research agendas. I will try to preserve the situated nature of the data, rather than just present it as existing together within a vacuum. Nevertheless, one of the problems in the field of educational research is the production of multiple atomized studies which are never brought together. In juxtaposing my different research studies and allowing them to interrogate and illuminate each other I hope to develop new understandings of the cross-cutting issues of learning, belonging, community and imagined social capital in ways that are not possible using only one study. Common themes and concerns have emerged and bringing these participants together and analysing these themes across the data has proven an interesting and productive move.

## Overview of the book

The book works with the data from these four research studies to explore what they reveal about learning communities and how they facilitate the development of the concept of imagined social capital. Analysis of anonymized data from the learners is woven throughout the book and all of the participants have been given pseudonyms.

In Chapter 1 my purpose is to start my analysis by exploring the concepts of 'self' which underlie the ways in which learners' lives are understood. Here I trace three dominant modes of thinking about the self that cluster around the notion of 'identity': what I call the 'authentic self' and the 'inescapable self' and what Francis and Skelton (2008) call the 'self-made self'. In opposition to these conceptualizations I suggest that there is no such thing as self, only an 'unself' that exists in flux. Learners' relations to these constructions of self are then explored. I proceed to discuss what the implications are for educational practices, how difficult it can be to break from the notion of 'identity' and what the benefits might be of doing so in a systematic way. This chapter discusses the ubiquity of voice and narrative in research on adult learners and their limitations as vehicles with which to explore the unself. It also engages with current debates about 'emotion', arguing for a cultural approach to representing what we know as 'feelings'.

I then move forward in Chapter 2 to critique the ways in which the idea of catering for a unified self via establishing unified learning communities has been dominant in educational thinking. I question the innocence and desirability of 'learning community', positing instead Iris Marion Young's idea of the 'unoppressive city' as a better model for educational institutions (Young 1990). The concept of 'communities of practice' is also explored, with discussion of how this has taken on a prescriptive rather than descriptive role in the field of adult learning. I explore how attempts to impose learning communities are often resisted and negated by learners and unpick the problematic aspects of communities of practice for marginalized people.

In Chapter 3 I proceed to argue that what I have termed 'imagined social capital' plays a more important role in generating belonging than forming learning communities or communities of practice does. I outline my concept of 'imagined social capital' as the benefits that accrue from symbolic and imagined networks and argue that these benefits are more productive than those produced in and through learning communities. The chapter explains how learners create imagined social capital for themselves from their own symbolic connections and networks and explores how this is linked to resistance. I demonstrate that imagined social capital can function in complex ways: by identifying the symbolic networks of 'what I am not'; by symbolic links with the natural world; by networks formed through nostalgia for a mythical past; by symbolic networks created to counter abjection. The various meanings of imagined social capital and how it relates to myth, nature, nostalgia and abjection are all discussed.

In Chapter 4 I then move to analyse how understanding belonging and the workings of imagined social capital could help to reshape educational spaces and ways of conceptualizing learning. I begin by exploring notions of home and belonging as they emerge in the learner accounts. The chapter then moves to investigate how learning operates in spaces outside of formal institutions, in particular focusing on informal learning among white working class men. I contrast this with constructions of space experienced in schools, colleges and universities and discuss the implications of 'smooth' and 'striated' space for educational practice. I conclude by tracing how current educational frameworks position many people as a 'waste of space' and how that is being actively resisted by learners themselves.

In Chapter 5 the notion of waste is replaced by a focus on what Lorraine Code (2006) terms 'ecological thinking': where everything can be used productively. The epistemological challenges raised by lifelong learning and the experiences of those in my studies provide a focus for this chapter. Recognizing that existing challenges to the 'masters knowledge', such as feminism, black feminism, queer theory and postcolonial theory, have not really disrupted the paradigm of what counts for valid knowledge in mainstream education, I try to move from theorizing *about* knowledge to theorizing *from* embodied joy of knowledge, drawing on ecological thinking. I explore how this approach, which recognizes the inter-connectedness of all things, can potentially transform solipsistic views of learning and knowledge into communal and holistic ones and explore the research data using this approach.

In the Conclusion I summarize the main findings of the book, reflect upon the conditions of its production and reflexively discuss the potential and the limitations of the idea of imagined social capital. I end by discussing the ways in which imagined social capital can best be facilitated.

To conclude this introductory chapter, I would like to acknowledge some debts and the role of others in the research projects I have conducted. In building my research, I have worked both alone and with different fellow researchers. In particular Liz Thomas, Kim Slack, Lorraine Casey, Katy Vigurs, Rob Lawy and Kim Diment have played key roles across these different projects. I want to recognize the vital importance and value of these research partnerships, but to stress that the responsibility for this book and the analysis and arguments within it is mine alone. This responsibility cannot be a claim to sole authority or to work without influences. I have been influenced by many people beyond those I have worked with directly, including those whose ideas have stimulated and inspired me over time such as Beverley Skeggs, Valerie Hey, Elspeth Probyn and Lorraine Code. Influences 'appear in a text . . . through the effects of alteration and operation they have produced in it. Debts cannot be transformed into objects either' (de Certeau, op. cit., p. 44) and so this text is hybrid and multi-generated, highly indebted and yet my own.

# Chapter 1

# Learning to Belong

## Conceptualizing the 'self'

Across all my work I am interested in our moves between the 'real' and the 'imagined' and the implications this has for learning. Such shifts are exemplified in Carol Ann Duffy's (1990) poem 'In Your Mind', where 'you' the reader take a long and vivid journey to a place where everything is strange and alluring but also familiar, 'apt' and 'yours': 'you are there, in the other country, knowing its name', only to find yourself simultaneously sitting at your desk watching 'the English rain'. Is it necessary to visit the 'other' country to gain an umbrella to shield one from the rain and provide the strength to carry on in the real world? With such multiple belongings and multiple locations how possible is it to locate where or who we are, or as Mary Gaitskill suggests, for others to recognize us?

> It's not an easy thing. If you can't find the right shape, it's hard for people to identify you. On the other hand you need to be able to change shape fast; otherwise you get stuck in one that used to make sense but that people can't understand any more.
>
> (Gaitskill 2008, p. 16)

As she argues, movement is also necessary to evade the possibility of self-entrapment and to ensure connection with others. Belonging thus can never be a process of sticking where we are. The question for this book particularly is what role learning plays in negotiating this process of belonging. In addressing these questions, I first need to establish the terms under which

I understand the learner and their self, which belongs or does not. This chapter explores a range of implicit assumptions about 'selfhood' that are prevalent in literature on lifelong learning, examining ways in which this self is conceptualized and the connections that are made between such a self and learning. In doing so, it seeks to critique dominant conceptions of 'identity' as employed in much of the literature on adults' learning. Despite the influences of poststructuralist thought, discussions of identity in this literature still seem to fall into conceptual traps. There are of course crossovers and multiplicities of positions, but I have found it useful to outline some broad trajectories.

 It is possible to discern three dominant strands of thinking. First, the notion of an authentic self, who we 'truly' are, only waiting to be set free, is a highly pervasive one in culture generally and in educational writing. This self is autonomous, in that it speaks only for itself; ultimately it is *the* source of meaning. This is exemplified by the discourse of voice, where education becomes a matter of 'finding a voice' to express the full potential of this authentic self. The duty of educators is thus framed as empowering students to speak and to do everything they can to 'listen to the voices of learners'. This trope can be found throughout the literature, and conferences and projects abound with 'voice' as their organizing principle. Voice takes on a powerful meaning which is political and even spiritual and it leads inexorably to a certain view of identity which is unquestioned, but ultimately naive and simplistic. The assumption is that voice coughs up identity: that a person speaks with a unified voice, that this voice can express the truth of the person and is a barometer of authenticity.

 Secondly we have what could be called the 'inescapable self'. Here more socio-cultural conceptions of identity concern themselves with the impact of factors such as gender, 'race' and class: seeing identity as strongly shaped by external forces, but once shaped somehow strongly bound by those experiences (see, for example, Reay 2001 and Hey 2003). This is identity as inescapable and embodied, moving with us wherever we go. This identity is not seen as 'true', in the sense of being a hidden self we are born with, but it is understood as imprinted and inexorable. This field of thought has developed a strong psycho-social dimension which argues that even when material conditions shift, a pervasive sense of shame about origins is left to haunt the self. Similarly, even though feminist poststructural theory is often employed to analyse how this self is constructed in and through discourse, the discussion still resolves around an outcome that could be recognized as an identity.

Educational thinking is strongly influenced by these conceptions of the authentic and the inescapable self, whether it manifests as a liberal desire to free the individual to attain the full flowering of their selfhood or whether it be a call to redress those factors which have produced disadvantaged and even damaged individuals. Both of these positions are extremely important. Indeed I count myself as one who has both wittingly and unwittingly adopted both perspectives in my work.

A third way of thinking about identity is what Francis and Skelton (2008) have called 'the self-made self', grouping together 'reflexivity theorists' such as Bauman, Beck and Giddens with the work of Judith Halberstam. Here the self is a 'project' worked on over time and not limited by either structure or biology: 'the self is to some extent freed from social structures . . . and able . . . to make itself' (Francis and Skelton, p. 319). This emphasis on individuation in contemporary society (Beck and Beck-Gernsheim 2002) and the idea that we are all engaged in making sense of our lives through reflexive narratives of the self (Giddens 1991) is both widely influential and strongly contested. It has been argued that this is a luxury most open to those who are white and middle class with most to gain from the process of individuation (Ribbens-McCarthy *et al.* 2002). As I have discussed elsewhere, it does not reflect the realities of provincial living, moreover, trauma and alienation make it impossible for many people to create such narratives (Quinn 2003a). Similarly, Francis and Skelton (2005) point out that the freedom to perform such self-made selfhoods as Halberstam's 'masculine femininity' may be radically constrained by the prejudice and violence of others. However, there is a further discussion that Francis and Skelton (2005) do not pursue. Contingent on theorizations of the 'self-made self' is the belief that there is a culminating identity which can be expressed and encapsulated. It may set new boundaries around that selfhood, but the self remains a bounded object.

4    A fourth way of thinking about identity is that it does not exist. This is what we could call the unself: subjectivity engaged in a perpetual process of flux, so that, unlike the self-made self, there is never anything so concrete as an identity emerging. Such a concept does not neglect the significance of material or discursive forces, but suggests that this is an ongoing process and there is no cutting through at any point to reveal either an authentic, inescapable or even self-made self:

> . . . the subject is not an 'entity' or thing, or a relation between mind (interior) and body (exterior). Instead it must be understood as a series of flows, energies, movements and capacities, a series of fragments or segments capable of being linked together in ways other than those that congeal it into an identity.
>
> (Grosz 1994, pp. 197–8)

In her research on women artists and education, Maria Tamboukou tries to elaborate the idea that there is no fixed moment of selfhood or identity: 'In following Deleuze-Guattarian (1980/1988) lines of flight I am considering the self as a threshold, a door, a becoming between multiplicities, an effect of a dance between power and desire' (Tamboukou 2008, p. 361). She provides a rare example of educational research which convincingly tries to break free of the authentic, the inescapable and the self-made self. In general, although the more postmodern perspective of the unself certainly exists within the educational community, in my view it is not applied consistently. There are many feminist post-structuralist writers, for example, who carefully unpick discourses and performances, inspired by theorizations from Butler and Foucault. Nevertheless, in postulating these intersections, they also discuss their subjects as having identities that can be spoken about and understood. The concept of identity reasserts itself and generally the dream/nightmare of the authentic or inescapable self is not foregone. Just to quote one recent example, in her latest book, *Learning Spaces*, Maggi Savin-Baden stresses the importance of fluidity, but still links this to 'identity' and to the production of an authentic 'voice' which is seen to belong to that identity (Savin-Baden 2008).

Another problem is that discussions employing a postmodern perspective on subjectivity do not necessarily follow it through by conducting research or analysing empirical data. For example, in *Novel Education*, part of a series on postmodern theories of education, Deborah Britzman employs a typically oblique relationship to empirical data where she uses 'my interpretations of the reconstruction of our interaction', to tell the story of a discussion with a student teacher. She unpicks this moment as the fulcrum of a detailed analysis of 'a pedagogical fact' (Britzman 2006, p. 206, pp. 166–71), rather than drawing on data generated from a research study. One explanation for this approach is that if there is no authentic self then there is no advantage in generating rich voice-centred data. Britzman's practice also has illustrious antecedents. De Certeau discusses how Foucault and Bourdieu write stories, and how the folktale, the recounted practice, is a model of scientific enquiry. He even stresses (in terms which Britzman's title echoes) 'the theoretical value of the novel' (de Certeau 1984, p. 78). However, my argument would be that rich empirical data is supremely useful, not in providing access to real selves via the medium of voice, but in providing a multi-layered outcrop of the processes whereby a subjectivity in flux is shaped and reshaped and the role that cultural narratives play in that shaping. It is a particular and evocative starting point for exploration of these movements. A tale told at remove, however fascinating the narrator, is ultimately no substitute.

What I will try to do in this book is to take hold of this very slippery concept of the learner as unself in flux and analyse my empirical data in the light of this understanding, thinking through the implications for discussions of 'learning community'. Nevertheless, for reasons I shall discuss, I fully expect not to succeed in this project and that other more dominant conceptualizations of identity, such as the authentic and inescapable self, will continually ambush my narrative. There are many reasons why it is difficult to unyoke from such dominant concepts of identity. On a personal level, the concept of an authentic self is deeply comforting, so much so that resistance seems counter-intuitive. As the novelist and literary theorist Siri Hustvedt argues:

We need to think of the self as a continuum, as a steady story over time.

The mind is always searching for similarities, associations, repetitions because they create meaning. When recognisable repetitions are disrupted, people say, "He wasn't himself" . . . It's the feeling or impression of foreignness that makes us want to cast off the interruptions, explosions, lapses, and inconsistencies – all the material in ourselves that we refuse to integrate into a narrative.

(Hustvelt 2006, p. 205)

Without the security of having a self, we may be frightened of the emptiness that is left, what Jenny Diski calls: 'an agony of lack of self . . . just the echoing vacancy of a shallow vessel, an empty container, with nothing evident in it at all; its perfect hollowness is merely assuaged temporarily by inputs of reading, music or television' (Diski 2006, p. 213).

The idea of a unified subject with integral values is also so embedded in humanist discourse that it is completely naturalized. Cultural forms surround us, beckoning us to uncover our 'true' identity and with it security and happiness. Paradoxically becoming the 'real me' or the 'me I was meant to be' legitimizes multiple attempts at self making, from breast implants to gender reassignment surgery. More challenging still is the reconciliation of personal flux with conditions of material stasis. While the unself is in flux, the conditions within which this is enacted are all too often ones of stasis, limitations, structural barriers and inequalities, which make movement very difficult, as I shall discuss. However, unlike the inescapable self which can never ultimately elude structuring forces, the unself is not materially bound. Fluidity can exist at the level of the symbolic and imagined, as I discuss in Chapter 3.

The self-made self is also one that is difficult to evade, because it is driving rhetoric and practice in education. It is not just a question of being 'who you are', because contentment with one's state is portrayed as being inadequate and lacking in aspiration. A person must be the best they can be, achieve their personal potential and as such be the right kind of citizen. In the UK, education and citizenship are absolutely and explicitly linked, from citizenship classes at school to the assertion that higher education makes people more engaged citizens: 'HE also brings social benefits . . .

there is strong evidence that graduates are more likely to be engaged citizens' (DfES 2003a). The most pervasive discourse in this context is that of 'waste', applied to those who are not learning as much as they should be and thus refusing the mantle of citizenship, and I shall return to this issue in Chapter 4. Changing and perfecting the self is both individualistic and socially responsible and the upwardly mobile self is perceived as hopefully moving their family and community up with them. The self-made self, who holds the power to make themselves whatever they want to be, and is not constrained by either inner or outer forces, is a tantalizing proposition. It stands in opposition to a self who is essentially vulnerable and fragile and requires therapeutic interventions in the guise of education to prop itself up (Ecclestone and Heyes 2008). Freedom, agency and self-reliance become the watchwords and the self-made self is left to cut its own swathe through the world: a fantasy figure of wish-fulfillment.

The inescapable self has a strong pull in the opposite direction and in some respects is the most difficult to relinquish of all. It evokes a sense of solidarity with those who share similar inequalities and a political drive to work together to redress them. It positions itself as counter to the neo-liberal (and self-made) ideal that with the right aspirations and personal power anything can be achieved and thus provides a counterpoint to the dominant educational policy discourse of deficit and waste. Without the work that has stemmed from this position much of our critical knowledge about learning and education would be lost.

However, in making identity the mantra and core of discussion, all of these three positions of authentic, inescapable and self-made self tend to move us towards a cul de sac from which it is difficult to move. Drawing on the unlikely ally of the romantic poet and thinker Samuel Coleridge, I want to employ his famous distinction between fancy and imagination in *Biographica Literaria*. According to Coleridge:

imagination . . . dissolves, diffuses, dissipates, in order to recreate . . . It is essentially *vital*, even as all objects (as objects) are essentially fixed and dead.

Fancy, on the contrary, has no other counters to play with but fixities and definites . . . it must receive all its materials ready made from the law of association.

(Coleridge 1975 edn, p. 167)

Ultimately, like fancy, the authentic, inescapable and self-made selves can only deal with fixities and definites, because they produce recognizable identities, objects which move in recognizable pathways across the board game of life. The unself, however, is not an object and cannot be employed as such, as it is constantly dissolving, diffusing and recreating, never, as Grosz (1993) puts it, 'congealing' into identity. What Coleridge terms the 'vitality' of imagination can also be seen in the energy of the unself. An unself, which is potentially anything (or nothing) at all but is being constantly constructed and reconstructed by material forces, enables us to hold simultaneous conceptions of transformation and recognitions of oppressions. This opens up different visions of what learning can be and what stands for knowledge.

## Learners' ideas about self

*I'm thinking about the 'educated person'. I realise that the idea that knowledge comes from everywhere and the idea that the person is not fixed and complete are intertwined . . . On the bus sun shines through the trees and things feel good now.*

*(J. Q., research diary)*

Having discussed how educational researchers conceptualize self, how do learners talk about this issue? In analysing my empirical data it seems that it is not a question of dividing up the different concepts of self and assigning them to different groups, but that they emerge and cross over in multiple ways amongst the same person. Nevertheless, dominant trends do seem to emerge within particular studies. I have found that the notion of the authentic and voice-centred self had particular resonance for participants, especially when linked with education. For example, the working class women university students I studied presented themselves in most contexts in terms that befit postmodern intellectuals. They rejected notions of essential womanhood:

> 'we don't go round with headbands on saying "woman" . . . you can't just say women are one way and men are another. There's not just two genders anymore, everything is so mixed now – there's any number of combinations.'
>
> (Julie Ann, focus group)

They saw themselves as of necessity playing multiple roles in multiple contexts. Part of their construction, particularly for working class women, was that they were not entitled to a self. 'Self' was a performance played for the benefit of others, for example in the family or at work. However, education was connoted as the sphere where they might make selfhood claims. It was when talking about their learning that notions of authenticity emerged, emotively, often with tears, with phrases such as: 'this is *me* coming out' (Carole).

For those students who had dropped out of university any stories of regret so often focused on a perceived betrayal of this authentic self and its intrinsic values.

> I am not a person who leaves things. I can't come this far just to chuck it away. I am not that kind of person. I was heartbroken. I was really sad and I thought it was the end of my life.

This is the double bind of 'authenticity': the idea of authentic selfhood is a cultural narrative, yet when it surfaces it exhibits the tropes of the real and the inner.

The inescapable self is also called up by many of my participants, particularly those in the study of working class dropout, who present their educational experiences as fundamentally shaped by their early experiences of disadvantage:

I think that people in the valleys they haven't got much confidence as a
community you know . . . you get a sense of being knocked down and your
family is the same you know, not good enough, not good enough . . . we're
told not to make a fool of yourself in front of other people.

(Female student who had dropped out of university in Wales)

This inescapable self is forced to repeat the patterns of the past in every
context it finds itself, including higher education. However, as this quote
demonstrates, it is essentially dependent on anticipating an audience primed
to reject or look down on it. Thus its natural behaviour is a performance. This
very artificiality calls into question how immutable this selfhood really is.

Discourses of the self-made self appear to shape the perceptions of the
young people in the study on jobs without training and to affect the way they
want to present themselves. So, even in situations where the inescapable self
might be evoked there are also struggles to assert the capacity to shift and
reshape. Charmaine, whose parents were only 14 when she was born, who
has had a troubled adolescence and now lives in a homeless hostel, seems
to be in a hopeless situation:

Interviewer: Are you still living with your mum?
Charmaine: No.
Interviewer: You're not now?
Charmaine: No.
Interviewer: Oh. OK what happened there?
Charmaine: I got kicked out.
Interviewer: Again?
Charmaine: Yeah.
Interviewer: No, oh dear.
Charmaine: I know. I'm living in a bed and breakfast . . . So it depends what
    happens really. It's like my life has taken a drastic turn, I suppose.
Interviewer: I remember when we spoke before you had had a terrible
    time you know because you had been kicked out when you were 15
    and then you kind of got back on your feet and do you feel oh well it's
    all gone wrong again?

Charmaine: Yeah I've been doing like bad things.

Interviewer: Like what?

Charmaine: Drugs and drink.

Interviwer: Drink and drugs well they tell me there is a big thing here in Weston really.

Charmaine: Yeah and I just got in with the wrong crowd and I have been drinking drugs and I am addicted to shoplifting.

Nevertheless Charmaine defiantly resists her 'destiny' and claims that she herself by her own actions and force of will can change the future:

Charmaine: Yeah I don't like to predict the future because you can change it.

Interviewer: What, you think you personally can change the future? How can you do that?

Charmaine: By doing the right choices.

Interviewer: Um.

Charmaine: That benefit you and people around you.

Interviewer: What if you make the wrong choice in life?

Charmaine: You can go back.

Interviewer: Yes.

Charmaine: Don't ever think that you are stuck in a dead end because you can just pull yourself up. It's like people like on a world basis you could easily get onto heroin or something and think you are in a dead-end world but all they have to do is bring themselves up and see a psychiatric help and get themselves up and get a job.

These images of choice, of redressing mistakes, of pulling the self up from even the most difficult circumstances by means of therapy and work ethic turn the tables on the interviewer, and place Charmaine temporarily in the controlling position. 'Stuck in a dead end' is exactly where policy makers perceive Charmaine and others like her to be, but the self-made self (theoretically) does not have to belong anywhere it doesn't want, it can always move on. Undercutting the rhetoric of self-help, however, is the deep sadness of poverty, struggle and desperation.

For the unself, there is nothing that is permanent and it is much less possible to draw on bravado and self-belief: 'The spiralled being who, from outside, appears to be a well-invested center, will never reach his center. The being of man is an unsettled being which all expression unsettles' (Bachelard 1994, p. 214). Unsurprisingly, amongst my participants this is thrown most into relief in the narratives of those who are materially most insecure, such as the homeless people:

> What a lot of people have got to wake up to is that it can happen to anyone. I'm 33 years old now, five years ago I was a fully qualified chef . . . now look at me, it can happen to anybody . . .
>
> (Alan)

However, there are other ways in which this 'unsettled being' is revealed. For example for the students who had dropped out, the rightness or wrongness of this decision and their personal relation to it oscillated over time:

> When I left I was relieved, I had it niggling away at me that I didn't want to be there. Looking back now I don't know if I regret it. One of the boys who was doing the same course as me lives in the same street as me. We have been friends all our lives, he is in his last year now. I do think sometimes if I'd only stuck at it . . .
>
> (Ann)

> When I left I thought perhaps I ought to have stayed. Maybe. But given time now I feel I have done the right thing. Now I can just move on and do what I need to do.
>
> (Lucy)

The interesting point here is that this uncertainty and flexibility of the unself is not seen as a legitimate position. It is a liability not to know or set fixed boundaries for the self and this must be policed and punished.

Non-retention is 'setting students up to fail' and 'unacceptable' (DfES 2003b). The Higher Education Funding Council for England (HEFCE) has been tasked with 'bearing down' on those institutions that allow it to happen (DfES 2003b) and is currently doing so in a draconian fashion. The post-compulsory nature of higher education accentuates this notion of compliance. Zembylas and Fendler (2007), have argued that:

> current educational discourses make it possible for us to accept a definition of freedom that means the same thing as self governance. We have become free to be normal, and it would not be normal to act in defiance of community norms.
>
> (Zembylas and Fender 2007, p. 328)

Going to university is normal and leaving early is an aberration. It is possible to conceptualize the young people in our study of dropouts as unruly unselves, rather than as inadequate unified identities. Part of this unruliness stems from non-linear understandings of what learning lives are or can be. This they share with other young people who step outside of normalized educational pathways, such as the young people in jobs without training. For these subjects, measurements of success do not fit regular patterns. Nevertheless, they cannot ultimately escape the penalties that ensue when community norms are flouted: 'Because they [student dropouts] haven't got a recognized skill or previous job they're not allowed to restrict their job choices and must accept the minimum wage. It's almost as if "I'm down and you're keeping me down here."' (Job Centre Plus adviser, Research Jury Day)

The students who had withdrawn early found it very difficult to return to education or to move on to find jobs. The higher education system does not lend itself to spiralling selves who keep changing their minds. It is not an asset to have what Keats called 'negative capability': the ability to live within uncertainties.

In all of these discourses of selfhood and learning, different problems emerge. My contention is that until we move beyond our perpetual focus on the authentic, inescapable or self-made self we cannot access the transformational potential of learning. If the purpose of learning is to free the authentic self, then it has a finite moment of release. If its purpose is to counteract the problems endured by the inescapable self, then it will be doomed to failure. If it is just a tool for the self-made self then it is a solipsistic endeavour. If, however, it is in tune with the unself, it offers an endless spiral of possibility, for: 'it is better to live in a state of impermanence than in one of finality' (Bachelard, op. cit., p. 61). An unself is never finished and it is happy that way. It doesn't have to spend forever searching for the authentic self just out of reach, mourning the pangs of the inescapable self, or striving to be a self-made self. It is free to dream and always open to learning new things.

I would argue that we are all always lost in transition, not just in the sense of moving from one task or context to another, but as a condition of our subjectivity. This vision of life as permanent flux is a celebration of risk and uncertainty, an energetic conception of subjectivity which seeks to free it from the limiting constraints of personhood. With such a dynamic conception of transition comes a freedom from fixating on fixed moments of change. If educational policy makers were to adopt this model, the current fetishization of the certain time frames and activities, such as the 14–19 curriculum or widening participation for the under 25s, would make way for an emphasis on flexible, 'unsettled' and spiralling movements throughout a learning life.

We constantly change, we transform, we move backwards and forwards, we do not coalesce either before or after even the most momentous life crisis. There is no such thing as an identity, nor a discrete moment of transition – only subjectivity and flux. This is the strength of our condition, not a weakness, for policy makers enjoy the gateway notion of transition, because it synchronizes with their vision of a pathway along which learners can be led to goals that are predefined, neat and orderly. This is closely tied with a vision of the person as an integrated, identifiable, and thus manageable, citizen. Subjectivity and learning are not so compliant, but where there is chaos there is also creativity. Education should mirror the flux of our being, rather than trying to subjugate it with rigidity.

## Belonging and education

> Staring out through the windshield, off into the horizon, Abby began to think that all the beauty and ugliness and turbulence one found scattered through nature, one could also find in people themselves, all collected there, all together in a single place. No matter what terror or loveliness the earth could produce – winds, seas – a person could produce the same, live with the same, live with all that mixed-up nature swirling inside, every bit. There was nothing as complex in the world – no flower or stone – as a single hello from a human being.
>
> (Lorrie Moore 2009, p. 95)

What does this challenge to the validity of 'identity' as an organizing concept do to the notion of belonging and education? An authentic model of self-hood implies that there is a right place for this person to be, a true home in which the true self can belong. In writing on the lives of students and academics at elite universities the notion that someone has 'found their spiritual home' is a common leitmotif. All the authentic self has to do is find that safe harbour. In contrast, a socially constructed model of identity, of the inescapable self, concerns itself with barriers and exclusions: the ways in which the learner, because of their background, feels alienated from educational institutions. It is common to find a rhetoric in new universities which anticipates this alienation and reassures the student that these fears and barriers are being actively addressed. A self-made self takes advantage of new freedoms of individuation in order to stake a claim not just of belonging, but of possession of educational institutions. What ties all these concepts together is belief that belonging is desirable and necessary for learning to take place.

However, if flux is taken as the organizing principle, then this need to belong is displaced by a need to move, to change. Learning becomes less associated with a place where one can fit than an openness to multiple spaces – a lifelong learning: 'What is critical in the experience of freedom is our movement in between (starting and finishing), when we follow lines of flight or escape, the intermezzo, the process of becoming other' (Tamboukou, op.

cit., p. 361). So is it possible to shift the discourse away from settlement to movement in order to understand belonging in a radically different way?

## Nomads and compasses

One figure which may help in fusing together becoming and belonging is the 'nomad'. There has been detailed discussion in feminist literature about the generative notion of the nomad, and the opportunities it offers to escape being pinned down by limiting categories and practices (Braidotti 1994). For Helen Colley (2007), however, this feminist nomad figure is imbued with privilege. She notes that Braidotti's examples are artists, writers and middle class women and places against this dream of the nomad the harsh reality of being a refugee. This injunction to remember materiality and the shaping of movement by oppression and inequality is well-founded. However, I am not willing to abandon the potency of perpetual movement altogether, and so I want to turn to M. Jacqui Alexander's image of 'Crossing', which potentially addresses the material suffering which troubles Colley. The image of 'crossing' partly evokes the enforced Atlantic crossing of Africans into slavery in the USA, but:

> is also meant to evoke/invoke the crossroads, the space of convergence and endless possibility; the place where we put down and discard the unnecessary in order to pick up that which is necessary. It is that imaginary from which we dream the craft of a new compass.
>
> (Alexander 2005, p. 8)

Crossing, for Alexander, simultaneously symbolizes both the enforced consequences of empire and imperialism but also our potential capacity to move into new possibilities. So we are neither totally free nor totally enslaved by history. A new materialism does not encompass us but neither can we dismiss the materiality of oppression and inequality. Alexander uses the image of the compass in her work in both senses, as in the compass that shows bearings and as the compass that draws an arc. This metaphor leads me further to the poet Janet Frame (2008) whose life and work also potently enfolds both deep suffering and imaginative escape, as she successfully used her writing to negotiate an existence often spent in mental hospitals. In her poem 'Compass' she too is drawn to the image of the compass and asks the reader if they would rather be the sharp centre or the 'wandering foot': that which stays at home, or that which moves. Her resolution is to reject both positions in favour of being: 'The radius tasting every drop of distance'. It is the radius itself, the arc of crossing that matters here, and this encapsulates the movement, the possibility that Tamboukou (2008) also talks about in her work. If nomad is less a physical move than a state of mind – an imaginative possibility – then anyone can be one. If the nomad and the compass tell us something important about our everyday rootlessness it may cure us of a futile search for roots. In my view belonging should be about moving forward as an unself open to change, not constantly looking back, tracing family histories and creating personal mythologies in an attempt to fix and excavate identity.

## Researching voice and story

Images of crossing and compasses are all very well, but how do we work with them in trying to understand the lives of learners? Researching the unself poses particular problems. If there is nothing so solid as an identity what are we connecting with when we conduct research with participants and how do we represent them in any meaningful way? This is an issue that has concerned me throughout my research. My conclusion has been that if we are analytical and proceed from a position where we deconstruct what is said, rather than taking what they say at face value, then research based on voice is just as meaningful as research based on any other human manifestation. There is nothing immutable – even the rocks we stand on – and no knowledge claims can be based on fixity. In having my participants' utterances I need not delude myself that I have captured their souls or any kind of 'self'. For many researchers, facing up to the problems and limits posed by voice-centred narrative is a live issue (see, for example, Doucet and

Mauthner 2008). The precise status of the story told by a participant is always under debate, with a radical uncertainty emerging as the most convincing position on this issue:

> Whatever else a story is, it is not simply the lived life. It speaks all around the life: it provides routes into a life, lays down maps for lives to follow, suggests links between a life and a culture. It may indeed be one of the most important tools we have for understanding lives and the wider culture they are part of. But it is not the life, which is in principle unknown and unknowable.
>
> (Plummer 1995, p. 168, quoted in Doucet and Mauthner, ibid.)

However, despite these theoretical recognitions that the relationship between narration and life is a tenuous and artificial one, it seems that educational research often proceeds in practice as if narration is the unveiling of a self. In both research and pedagogy in adult learning there has been great faith in the power of individual 'stories' in allowing the true self to be recognized and validated and thus move on constructively (see, for example, Merrill and West 2009).

Narrative has also been posited as itself constituting a site for learning:

> By narrative learning we mean that learning can take place as a result of articulating stories from one's life, through the process of talking about and reflecting on life experiences, in other words from the very narration of one's biography; and can take place as a result of presenting stories from one's life, by having stories with content and structure, by having a narrative that says something about what and how you have learned. Narrative and narration are not simply a vehicle for such learning processes but can be understood as 'site' for learning.
>
> (Tedder and Biesta 2009, p. 89)

Yet, as I know very well, 'there are some stories that cannot be told, and some emotions that cannot be expressed' (Zembylas and Fendler, op cit, p. 328). The yoking together of the speakable with selfhood and education inevitably leaves those with lives that are marginal and incoherent or histories that are traumatic and aberrant, unable to make the transition to fully 'educated person'. They cannot use narrative as a site for learning.

The meaning of silence needs attending to. It is no coincidence that the students who had dropped out of university often felt unable to speak: 'Nobody realized there was anything wrong and nobody asked'. Being able to speak is seen as a sign of personal and educational good health:

> we try to make sure that young men feel that they are welcomed and treated seriously as artists when they arrive, you know someone like Ally is a good example, he was extremely shy when we first met him and now he's really quite self-possessed, self-aware, quite open, quite positive, talks about his range of skills . . . when we first met him he was extremely withdrawn and unsure about himself; he was very isolated really.
>
> (Paul, tutor, youth community arts project)

It is notable that the tutor here frees up speech, not by excavating Ally's personal life and what he is, but by focusing on what he can do and taking those skills seriously. It might be argued that this is a more ethical position than the confessional mode. There is something punitive about expecting people to freely tell the stories of their lives to more powerful others, and of course Foucault (1980) alerts us to the dangers of the confessional. There is also something paternalistic/maternalistic about it, which often places the listener in a quasi-parental position. Feminists have alerted educationalists to the use of silence as a form of resistance in the classroom and the same can be true in research contexts. Some participants may refuse to tell a story that can be comprehended and then used to restrict and pigeonhole them. Many of the young people in the jobs without training study, for example, were highly aware that their story of leaving school with few qualifications and now being engaged in low status jobs did not fit the narratives socially sanctioned for young people. Their response was often to create a life-narrative that could not be pinned down and seemed to traverse time and space in confusing ways. Their accounts shift spatially and temporally, making them very difficult to locate:

> George:  I lived in Swindon till I was 15 and then I moved away on my own.
>
> Interviewer:  Did you?
>
> George:  Yeah moved down to Bournemouth and I lived with my girlfriend.
>
> Interviewer:  Did you go to school there?
>
> George:  No, I went to work in a warehouse and got a supervisor's job there.
>
> Interviewer:  What, when you were 15?
>
> George:  I got it when I was 16.
>
> Interviewer:  So did you stay on at your secondary school in Swindon to take your GCSEs or not?
>
> George:  I did GCSEs there. I was back and forth when I was in Bournemouth.

They are vague about their job histories:

> Interviewer:  How many jobs have you had since you left school?
>
> Nathalie:  Between eight and ten.
>
> and mystify their qualifications:
>
> Interviewer:  What subjects did you take?
>
> Harry:  GCSE Rural Science, Financial Maths and managing money.
>
> Interviewer:  What GCSEs did you do?
>
> George:  English I got two Es – no that's Science I got two Es. I got English an E. Maths I did terrible. I got a D in Theatre Graphics and Design. Used to do Cooking but didn't actually take that but I could have done.
>
> Interviewer:  So in total how many did you get then?
>
> George:  That's a tough question. I wouldn't know.

The lines between fantasy and fact are kept blurred, or crossed and recrossed. Ball *et al.* (1999) suggest many young people conjure an 'imagined future' that bears little or no relation to the reality of their lives. The sheer refusal to make a convincing narrative is particularly marked in young people: this is not peculiar to the young people in the JWT cohort (Lawy 2002; 2006), but it is exacerbated by their negative social positioning. Our explanation for this was not that young people in JWT have some individual pathology, but that no socially validated narrative exists which will allow them to make their case. In a society where the onus is on gaining school level qualifications, continuing in education, getting a respectable job with training or somehow circumventing the system and gaining celebrity, those who do not do any of these things are losers, and no one wants to hear their story. Being vague on the details enables the young people to slip some of these constraints and evade being fixed. For the young people in our study the *present* itself was imaginary; little wonder therefore that formal transition points such as leaving school or interviews for jobs are slipped over and have little meaning and their narratives challenge any attempt to excavate a unified story of a coherent self.

So given all the issues of voice and silence, and the opportunities and pitfalls of identity-based narrative research, how possible is it to do justice to the unself in a research context? Tamboukou has conducted fascinating research into narrative, drawing on letters, documents, texts and interviews pertaining to the genealogy of women artists. Her argument is that instead of being hemmed in by temporality and linearity we should see narrative as tracing lines of flight: 'Rather than representing lives or subjects, narratives emit signs of how subjects respond to real and imagined experiences: they are both discursive effects and sites of discursive production' (Tamboukou, op. cit., p. 361). She is interested in:

> the how of spatial practices, rather than the psychologization of those practices and their connection to a particular character or persona. This approach makes connection with the Deleuzian concept of the individual as a plane wherein thought takes place as an event and not necessarily as a conscious process.
>
> (Tamboukou, op. cit., p. 362)

Although it could be argued that what she is tracing is a very particular 'plane', one that does have a subject-based goal – the creation of the self as a woman artist – this idea is transferrable to other groups of people. Bachelard provides an evocative image:

> . . . on the surface of being, in that region where being *wants* to be both visible and hidden, the movements of opening and closing are so numerous, so frequently inverted, and so charged with hesitation, that we could conclude on the following formula: man is half-open being.
>
> (Bachelard 1994, p. 222)

As a qualitative researcher my interest throughout is to see narratives not as marking the sites of flight of the perfectible self, but as cultural expressions very much shaped by cultural narratives at play around them. For example, in researching the young white men who had dropped out of university we do not see education making and shaping them into their real and perfect human form, but rather education being one of many sites where they act out certain culturally shaped roles. The young men in our study were involved in performances of whiteness and masculinity which drew on cultural narratives, such as nostalgia for the security and solidarity of 'lost' white jobs like pottery and mining. These cultural narratives and associated collective memories had a powerful effect on their behaviour and made it quite difficult for them to find security via education (see Quinn *et al.* 2006). Learners employ many interlocking narratives drawn from culture to make sense of and to justify their actions. Here, the story of the young working class man as rebel who does what he likes, casts a heroic gloss on leaving university early:

> The parents were not pleased when I left especially since my brother had done the same. They have learnt now that we will do what we want. As much as they try to help us, if we don't want to do it we won't do it.
>
> (student who had dropped out, England)

Conversely, the cultural narrative of the young working class man who acts on behalf of and in the name of the family, without consultation, makes dropping out an act of responsibility: 'My mum was upset when I left, but I think for her I had to leave, because there's no way she could have kept up the financial payments' (student who had dropped out, Scotland). Rather than telling the story of a 'self', I seek to unpick such cultural productions of the 'unself'.

## Self and emotions

The discussion on self, narrative and voice also feeds into some important current debates about emotion. As is so often the case, feminist pedagogy was way ahead of the field in addressing learning as an emotional issue (see, for example, Ellsworth 1989) and has been doing so for at least 20 years. The emotional costs of adults learning is hardly a neglected issue either. However, the emotion debate has accelerated into the mainstream of educational writing and become a major preoccupation. On one hand, there are those who predominantly ascribe educational problems to psycho-social issues of low self-esteem and argue for initiatives that promote emotional well-being and attention to the psychic needs of learners. They assume that emotions are ineluctably real and can be identified: 'Emotions such as fear, resentment and guilt, as well as enthusiasm, excitement and pride all infuse choice-making processes and help to explain the diversity of pathways young people take to university' (Christie 2009, p. 135).

In discussing 'learners' feelings', such as 'stress' and 'anxiety' (Robson *et al.* 2008, p. 319), the underlying belief appears to be that they will be able to put feelings into words and that when they do, these words provide access to raw emotion. Even those sophisticated writers such as Burman, who urge educational theory to move beyond such discussions of 'emotional literacy' and stress that: 'Rather than being *literate about* emotions the task is to *analyse the models of writing* emotions in circulation' (Burman 2008, p. 150, original emphasis), still seem to subscribe to the notion that there is something 'deep' and psychological called emotion. Taking a feminist psycho-social perspective, Leathwood and Hey (2009) exhort educators to work with emotions as conceptual tools: 'the investments, fears, pains, pleasures and contradictory emotions entangled within the world of education (enables an understanding of) how social and embodied forms of emotion shape the identities of subjects' (Leathwood and Hey 2009, p. 431).

Here again, despite the reference to 'social forms of emotion', emotion and 'identity' are held in a relationship of correspondence and both are represented as tangible realities.

On the other hand there are those who argue that a therapeutic ethos threatens to subsume more important educational and structural issues (Ecclestone and Hayes, op. cit.). From this perspective there has been a shift to prioritizing emotions over intellect and to stressing the fragility rather than the resilience of learners. For such writers, focusing on emotion is both dangerous and anti-educational. This position is characterized by a belief in an autonomous subject who can and should hold fundamental values and aspire to objective forms of knowledge.

The messy ground in between these two positions, where learners actually are, is little explored. Moreover, both positions neglect the culturally constructed nature of emotions and the extent to which they are not an unmediated slice of inner life. Tapping into emotion is seen as either desirable or exploitative, but either way the assumption is that the emotions are there openly available to manipulate for good or ill. The debate is also one about identity, with both positions assuming that there is something one might call a human subject that either needs protecting or needs freedom to express its own agency.

Sara Ahmed (2004) provides a powerful corrective in her postmodern analysis of the cultural and political meanings of emotion which responds to the condition of the unself:

> Sensations are mediated, however immediately they seem to impress upon us. Not only do we read such feelings, but how the feelings feel in the first place may be tied to a past history of readings, in the sense that the process of *recognition* (of this feeling or that feeling) is bound up with what we *already know*.
>
> (Ahmed 2004, p. 25)

To this I would add that naming something as a 'feeling' in the first place is in itself culturally mediated. A cultural analysis of emotions has not really permeated the educational literature and to access it, I have found it more productive to look to other forms of writing, such as this meditation on *Trying to Keep Still* by Jenny Diski:

> You remember X, then the feeling that belonged to it, or rather the feeling you attribute to it; catch the echo of that feeling and then step across that stepping stone to the next memory, or the next episode and if you can get it, its feeling. Add conversations, movies, fictions. Just occasionally you might, in the course of an hour or so, or an entire afternoon, suspect you had discovered some connected narrative . . . A pattern, a repetition, a process, an explanation. But like the burst of flavour of a single chocolate, the moment passes, what you thought you see fades and is forgotten or ungraspable.
>
> (Diski, op. cit., p. 215)

My argument would be emotions are negotiated states which come into being informed and regulated by culture and that are both formed by and perceived through layer upon layer of cultural accretions, as Diski's quote demonstrates. If we remove those layers, like stripping off the petals of a rose, there is nothing at the centre.

Cultural theory also helps us to understand that when we access a narrative what we often get is an act of witnessing, a twice-told tale rather than a fresh outpouring of authentic 'feeling': 'an act of telling and listening, performing and watching, it is, most important, an act of retelling or, in the language of performance, of 'twice-behaved behaviour' (Hirsch and Smith 2002, p. 9). Such ideas helped me to analyze how the women students in my study often told not their own stories but their mothers' stories of education, even though mothers were not the ostensible subject of enquiry. This even extended to speaking in different voices when summoning up the mother's story about educational losses and barriers, like an actress taking on a role:

> I went into nursing, I wasn't going to, I was going to go into art. My, my [stammering] mother was a nurse. She started in her 20s, they couldn't

start until they were 21. She had to wait and also she had to finish when she married, you know, so she never actually went back to it . . . Why did I have this thing I wanted to '*do it for her*' (spoken in a different deep voice) I don't know, I might have I don't really know.

(Grace, 62)

(see Quinn 2004b for full discussion)

So if we see patterns of emotion as cultural and political signs, and negotiations, not raw reality, how can this help us to read the learning lives of our participants? In an educational context such negotiation is shaped by prevailing ideas about what constitutes valid knowledge and acceptable ways of learning. Part of learning to belong is learning what emotions are acceptable to perform in whatever learning community. For example, in the academic community, vulnerability is not commonly considered an attribute, but in certain pockets, such as feminist research, admitting vulnerability has become a respectable, even desirable, performance. So if we see the parade of acceptable feeling and the suppression of unacceptable feeling as part of joining a learning community how does this manifest itself in the learners I am discussing?

For the women in university the regulation of emotion and its display was tied to discipline, so that in American Studies they might be asked to explore their own emotive response to texts and media, whereas in Environmental Studies the personal was seen as a liability, unless of course that personal was a rant against feminist ideas, as I shall discuss later. These different relations to the emotional and the personal were epistemological in nature. In Humanities one could not be expected to know unless one was prepared to feel. In the context of Science, feeling was a handicap to the purity of knowledge. When it comes to creative subjects, such as music and drama, intense emotional display is almost considered a prerequisite of valid learning, as the interviews with young men studying community music suggest:

I went to do a social science but actually music was just in my heart you know, I thought – that is what I want to do so even though I was doing very well at college I had to go. At the end of the day music is a sort of fulfillment where you have created something . . . it's your work, do y'know what I mean, there's nothing wrong or right about it . . . it belongs to you, it's like nurturing a child or something.

(Michael, community music organization)

In negotiating their way though institutions, learners in all my research studies seemed expected to deal in their own emotions as if they were cards in a game, suppressing them or laying them open as appropriate. If the emotions were laid out in front of the wrong person they seemed to fall flat: 'I went to see my tutor, I had tears, he said I should just leave' (young woman who had dropped out). Interestingly when appropriate sites of emotion were open, such as counselling services, they were often avoided. Most of the young people in the dropout study had never used such services, or even wanted to. It was as if they had evaded officially sanctioned sources of emotional support. They did not necessarily see themselves or early withdrawal as a problem and much of their reasoning was pragmatic:

I didn't find it an easy decision. I took lots of things into consideration. I didn't want to stay just for my friends. I wanted to do what was right for myself.

It just made me realise that there are other areas to be explored. For me, leaving was a positive experience.

They did not necessarily want to be cast as the vulnerable figure for whom everything was a struggle.

For those in the jobs without training study, being successful at work meant learning how to generate what were perceived as 'positive emotions' in relationships with others:

It makes you realize that GCSEs and stuff really don't affect what you do outside, workwise and dealing with real life situations, you realize there's a lot more stuff that's more important than grades. Getting a job really does depend on what sort of person you are and whether people can work with you.

(Liz)

Often this also involved avoiding expressing anger and resistance and accepting a pecking order. Liz, for example, accepted that being a young woman working in a car dealership placed her at the bottom of the hierarchy, even below a gay colleague who suffered sustained homophobic abuse: 'There's one guy who picks on me, he's a kind of bitchy gay guy. The others all call him "handbag", so he takes it out on me, but it's OK.'

The interviews conducted with these young people were very often characterized by silence, resistance, evasion, unwillingness to give themselves up. Many of them were monosyllabic. These were young people who had not succeeded in the school system and had not progressed to formal training or education post 16. Their formal education had been a process of closing down in the belief that others can't hear them and don't want to listen:

> When I was at school part of my depression was I was attacked . . . I met this woman who came out, this volunteer who was an old lady with hearing aids in both ears and she didn't listen to a word I'd said cause when I'd said something to her she'd try and change the subject and she just literally wouldn't listen and if I had something to say she'd interrupt and talk about what she wanted to talk about.
>
> (Jo)

To speak requires a listener willing to demonstrate understanding. The participants spoke far more in the second round of interviews and were surprised and pleased to find that the interviewer remembered them and the details of their lives. In terms of the linking of emotions with voice, in their accounts, particularly the young men, they moved the focus from the mouth to the hands, to the doing rather than the speaking and in a sense evaded the affective realm: 'I've got a practical mind . . . give me a book to learn, I can't learn it, tell me to do something, if I do it wrong, I know what I've done wrong straightaway, I can fix it like that' (John). 'Things at home that came to pieces, I could put them back together again' (Draco). This is perhaps because the affective is a classed and gendered zone and such young men learn frighteningly early that they don't belong in it. Loving learning (and having feelings about it) is something associated with successful middle class girls, not young working class men. They did love informal learning, as I shall discuss later, but as I have learned from experience, many people cannot accept the validity of love of learning for such men and this too they often kept hidden from public gaze.

These young people were aware that 'feelings', however problematic to negotiate, were a desirable and necessary part of belonging in the world. An extreme case was Charmaine, who, as discussed earlier, appeared to be retreating from her difficult life into drink and drugs. It is interesting that what concerned her about this was not criminality, or even her own vulnerability, but how it affected her capacity to care about others. She cared that she didn't care:

> I've changed a lot . . . for worse . . . I just don't care about feeling and I should . . . Three months ago maybe I wouldn't have thought it, it wouldn't have been like I don't care about no one . . . I wasn't doing drugs then . . . I don't do heroin or anything I don't want you to think that, just like weed and coke.

Charmaine's rather touching desire to protect her interviewer from the possible extent of her drug use seems to indicate that the caring discourse is still very powerful for her. It also suggests that emotions, whatever they are ontologically speaking, and however much generated by culture, still operate as palpable 'realities' in the lives of these learners. In exploring how people learn to belong, it is not that we should either celebrate or fear 'emotion', but that we should understand how we come to name something *as an emotion* and what the consequences of that naming are.

## Conclusion

In this chapter I have attempted to lay the ground for the rest of the book, by exploring the status of the 'who' that learns to belong. By problematizing identity, voice, narrative and emotion I am queering the grounds on which adult learners are commonly understood and written about. I argue that in addressing adult learners and their needs, common conceptions of the 'self' as being authentic, inescapable or 'self-made' are brought into play. These understandings inform educational practices and the approaches of researchers, policy makers, educators and learners. However, they lead us into a cul de sac. Conceptions of a fluid self do exist but they are not applied consistently and slippage into identity-talk happens all the time. This is understandable as identity is so culturally inscribed and the idea of an unself is so threatening. In asserting the significance of the fluid unself I do not intend to retreat into whimsy, but rather confront material practices. Proceeding with an idea of how I understand those who learn to belong and an aspiration to represent them in these fluid terms, I shall now move to consider how learning communities have been constructed to fit outmoded fixed concepts of learner, self and identity.

# Chapter 2

# Critiquing Learning Communities

Having unpicked the concept of the self, I will now turn to the ways in which education seeks to create homely communities in which that self can belong. Dominant conceptions of community are closely tied to humanistic notions of unified human subjects who have recognizable and bounded identities. Gereluk sums up the virtues of community as follows:

> Community is valuable for several reasons. The reasons range from aspects of belonging and attachment, to forming one's identity. Similarly community is often considered as a social good, developing dispositions of care, reciprocity and trust – all of which may have potential positive implications for individuals and society.
>
> (Gereluk 2006, p. 71)

Here community both creates and supports identity and it consists of a set of 'formed' individuals. Community brings together a number of unified selves to form a coherent whole, with its own unified identity. As discussed in Chapter 1, education is also understood to help form identity, thus community and education have a symbiotic relationship and are poised to work in harmony together for the good of the one and of the whole. As Webb and Warren (2009) demonstrate, educated individuals are held to be 'responsible learners' who will, by virtue of their acquisition of valuable skills, contribute to the common good: 'High level skills – the skills associated with higher education – are good for the individuals who acquire them and good for the economy. High level skills add value for all of us' (Department for Innovations Universities and Skills (DIUS) 2008: p. 3, quoted in Webb and Warren, op. cit., p. 52). This conjunction of education and community has become encapsulated in the concept 'learning community', which, like 'voice', is blandly ubiquitous. Ideally, it seems, our society should be one big happy learning community.

In this chapter I will demonstrate how I have critiqued the assumption of community as an unproblematic good, using the work of Iris Marion Young (1990), which explores how communities are created precisely on the backs of those who are not allowed to belong. In doing so I have deconstructed the notion of the innocence of community in educational settings, arguing instead that institutions should aspire to the status of what Young calls 'unoppressive cities', where people are allowed to be 'strangers' and there is no expectation of unity, either for self or group (see Quinn 2005a).

I will begin by discussing the pervasive concepts of 'learning community' and 'communities of practice' which are both highly influential at all levels of work on adult education. They permeate rhetoric about adult learning, from policy at national and institutional level to Mission statements and the daily concerns of practitioners. Every town, college, school and university it seems must aspire to be a learning community. Learning community has become a particularly familiar idea in higher education. In some contexts it describes innovative attempts to open up relationships between lecturers and students and there has been attention paid, particularly in the USA, to its role in the mechanics of facilitating learning by improvements to curriculum, assessment practices, etc. (see, for example, Leigh-Smith *et al.* 2004). There has also been a move to explore more closely how learning can be promoted within specific learning contexts (Edwards *et al.* 2009). This pedagogical focus is not what concerns me here. What interests me is the symbolic function of learning community as a blueprint of the pure institution and its status as an unproblematized good.

The following is a typical excerpt from the Mission statement of one of the universities in my study of 'dropout':

As an accessible learning community, we value inclusion and diversity and share the Government's commitment to increasing access and widening participation. We remain committed to ensuring that people from all backgrounds have the opportunity to study with us and we encourage a wider social mix. We work to attract learners with a wide variety of previous life and educational experiences.

(quoted in Quinn *et al.* 2005, p. 5)

It seems the idea of community is an idealized state for university and encapsulates its best vision of itself, which it then tries to sell to others. At its most exalted, captured in the following address to university lecturers, the university is transmuted into both heroic body and nurturing family: 'Universities should be bodies with great hearts as well as great minds. Our students are members of this community of learning and metaphorical sons and daughters to us all' (Ollin 2002).

If we look closely, the vision of 'learning communities' operating in dominant educational discourse is facile and retrogressive. Learning community is a mode of regulation and also a form of camouflage. A genealogy of 'learning community' in higher education in the UK shows that the term enters into public discourse corresponding to the massification and depersonalization of universities, while paradoxically trying to attest to their roots and to claim a form of historical validity. In the UK, universities have traditionally been seen as cloistered communities for reflection: indeed the value of the community was its elite exclusivity. Until comparatively recently, women, for example, particularly working class ones, were explicitly excluded. This discourse has now changed. The university is now posited as a community open to all of those with the will or ability to enter, even though, in reality, myriad forms of exclusion still operate through class, gender, disability, ethnicity and age (see, for example, Archer *et al.* 2003). So community becomes a yardstick by which people may measure their failure to belong.

Turning to adult education more generally, learning communities are envisaged as producing social capital, as in the resources generated by our relationships with others. Learning communities as sources and producers of social capital are a dominant image in UK policy thinking about adult education and lifelong learning more generally (see, for example, Learning and Skills Council 2003) and potentially include the kind of work and voluntary sector environments explored in my research studies. Learning communities are seen as places where social capital and learning can be maximized in a productive relationship between the social network and the learning context. In the UK, community sustains its idealized position in education, while operating for strictly pragmatic and regulatory ends. In adult education one emphasis has been on creating new types of learning communities in irregular spaces such as pubs. This is strongly linked to discourses of skill, employability, competition and citizenship with community placed at the heart of the government's social rhetoric. Ersatz community is created in order to create functioning citizen units. Former Prime Minister Tony Blair was famous for his overuse of community, for which he was mocked by a meeting of the Women's Institute (Whaley 2000) and this is a trait of current government and unlikely to change in the future. The university is posited as part of this network of learning communities, albeit with its own particular and privileged role to play. From being the quintessential site of reason, it is now 'but one player . . . in the knowledge game' (Barnett 2003, p. 161), a part rather than a pinnacle of the knowledge society. This encapsulates a precarious moment for the UK university. If, as Barnett (1997) argues, universities must shift from knowing as 'contemplation' to knowing as 'action', then part of this process is an explicit rather than implicit role in social inclusion and regeneration. The White Paper *The Future of Higher Education* spells this out quite categorically, stating that 'universities play a vital role in expanding opportunity and promoting social justice' (Department for Education and Skills, op. cit.). The idea of learning community seems to play a pivotal role in this process, and takes on a heavy burden for redressing inequality; but like motherhood and apple pie may not be as wholesome as it seems. As I shall discuss, rather than being conduits for social capital, learning communities can be prime sites for alienation.

## Communities of practice

I will move now to consider the concept of 'communities of practice', which I would argue is rather different in emphasis from learning community, but has also become highly influential. Learning communities are seen as entities that can be created artificially and with intent; they are the ideal towards which we must work. Communities of practice, however, have to grow incrementally, where community is built by the accretions of actions and events and shared understandings of what the task is and how to perform it: 'interconnected communities of practice through which an organisation knows what it knows and thus becomes, effective and valuable as an organisation' (Wenger 1998, p. 8). Where learning community is an idealized concept, it might be said that communities of practice is a pragmatic one; it is about what people do in their daily lives. It has been developed to describe the sorts of processes which go on within educational contexts and has also been used to understand how constructs such as gender become inscribed in and by common practices. A useful distinction between learning community and communities of practice might be that once made by Foucault (1980) between ideologies and procedures. Procedures, as in the daily work of communities of practice, are where 'the details overcome theory', while learning communities are rhetorical sites where 'ideology babbles on' (de Certeau 1984, p. 46). Nevertheless, in terms of educational policy and practice, both the concepts of learning community and communities of practice assume that 'community' is desirable. However we get there, it is somewhere where we must want to be.

The community of practice is built on shared conceptions of professionalism and a belief that there is a body of knowledge that new members can draw on and learn from. In a crossover moment with learning communities, it also resists fluidity and informality, by a process of what Wenger calls 'reification' (Wenger, op. cit.), where institutions take abstract ideas about their work and 'congeal' them into documents and symbols. In the community of practice there are expert practitioners and novices and thus hierarchical relationships. Above all there must be some belief that the practice in question is worthwhile and respectable. Having given talks about my research to many groups of practitioners involved in advising and supporting learners I have been struck by how this well-spring of belief overflows:

*Strangeness of so many people who can talk and talk – totally tapped into their practice – their reality – enviable? Is my unease sour grapes at not being part of*

*any recognisable community of practice, or is it a legitimate response to what seems*
*like complacency and self-congratulation?*

                                                    *(J. Q., research diary)*


It is indeed enviable to be so sure that our practices can be justified and are
correct, but the danger is that counter-arguments and practices become
located as unthinkable. The community of practice becomes self-protective
and self-perpetuating with its own language and mores:

> Librarian: I've been in meetings with college representatives and
> the only person who has talked about the learner as opposed to a
> funding unit is the librarian . . . you put them in an area meeting with
> representatives who are not from that culture and you know . . . I've
> been in a meeting with two representatives from the voluntary sector
> who've said virtually nothing and you can understand why . . . you
> might have four people from just a single college and three people
> from another college and two from a third college all talking the same
> college speak, all knowing exactly what they mean, all coming from
> the same academic background and you know what the result's going
> to be, you know that the people who aren't from that background,
> unless they're stroppy buggers . . . it's intimidating and you think well
> is this really to do with us and how do we get in here and how are our
> people not going to be disadvantaged by what's going on because it
> moves so fast, comments whiz round the table.
> Library Learning centre manager: Unless you are stroppy and you do
> ask and you don't mind appearing to be the class idiot it can be very
> difficult.
> (Focus group steering group, Library outreach project)

This is a vivid example of how the community of practice can unthinkingly
perpetuate its own power, even while trying to engage in partnership with
others. The idea of community of practice is a helpful one in that it pro-
motes understanding of how links are made by doing things in the same way

and together. However, what it fails to really address is how those things that the community of practice shares and values become transmitted to them – why these practices and not others, how are these practices culturally and politically shaped and what effects do they have on those not lucky enough to be enfolded in the community?

In the example above, those sharing a Further Education community of practice have become accustomed to calling a learner a 'funding unit'. Behind this habit lie a multitude of policy and social trends which shape the learning environment and there is nothing neutral, or voluntary, about buying into this community. The danger of this concept is that it becomes prescriptive not descriptive. Latterly it is seen as a tool whereby organizations can learn to be more effective. Wenger, for example, currently uses his ideas to conduct training and capacity building for academics around his concept of community of practice.

## Different perspectives on community

Two opposing views of community are found in the work of Vincent Tinto and Iris Marion Young and they provide a useful theoretical contrast in understanding the relationship between community and difference and in critiquing the concepts of learning communities and communities of practice that I have introduced. Young builds on feminist theorizing about the importance of differences such as race, gender and disability to problematize the comfortable and comforting notion of 'community'. She sees the idea of 'community' as potentially repressive and exclusionary: 'Community is an understandable dream . . . but politically problematic . . . because those motivated by it will tend to suppress differences between themselves, or implicitly to exclude from their political groups persons with whom they do not identify'.

She proposes another ideal in its place: 'the unoppressive city' which 'offers an understanding of social relations without domination in which persons live together in relations of mediation among strangers with whom they are not in community' (Young, op. cit., p. 303).

Tinto, an educational theorist who has been highly influential in the field of retention in higher education, presents a much more optimistic view, in that he has faith in community. His focus is on creating universities as places where students can thrive and feel they belong. He seems to elide differences and their consequences, and rather stresses that 'sharing' and 'connecting' can produce a community of equals. He argues that universities have a moral duty to develop communities which offer academic and social support and this is bolstered by the pragmatic imperative to retain students and ensure that widening participation is successful: 'the key concept is that of educational community and the capacity *to establish educational communities* that involve all students as equal members' (2003, p. 5, my italics).

My argument is that while much policy, practice and theorizing in the field of widening participation is driven by a Tinto-like vision, Young's ideas are actually closer to the ways in which students experience and re-imagine universities. In Tinto's ideal version of a learning community the pursuit of knowledge unifies and gives meaning to the collective experience. In practice both learning and community are assigned absolute and yet neutral value, an idealization that tends to prevent any exploration of their tensions and absence, including their gender or race tensions. At the same time community is brought to bear as a means of regulation. In the university itself it is interesting to see how learning community is used as a tool of purification and control. Typical of this is a consultative document *A Learning Community*, produced by a university which works hard to recruit and support 'non-traditional' students. The document employs 'learning community' as an idealized umbrella. Here potential problems of belonging and difference can be subsumed within a static discourse which is addressed to the student under the fixed headings: 'you are expected to' and 'you can expect'. The superficial cosiness of community is mordantly coupled with the admonitory subtitle: Making Knowledge Work.

One of the tasks of university new managerialism has been to create a spurious and unproblematized sense of shared community through such measures as mission statements, codes, symbols, corporate policy and procedures. However, step out of line from the community and expose practices that you cannot adhere to and you will be excommunicated, as various whistle blowers about academic standards have recently experienced in UK universities. Enforced community seems to make little contribution to developing a realm of ideas and in refusing to acknowledge difference and dissidence, in favour of purity and compliance, it simply serves to inhibit change:

> the polarisation between the impure, inauthentic society we live in and the pure, authentic society we seek to institute detemporalises the process of change because it fails to articulate how we move from one to the other. If institutional change is possible at all, it must begin from intervening in the contradictions and tensions of existing society.
>
> (Young, op. cit., p. 315)

This notion of purity and authenticity which Young questions here returns us to the discussion about authentic selves. Although, as I have indicated, respecting rather than trying to gloss over difference is crucial, this is a sensitive and complex process. Those who do try to address inequalities within communities often run the risk of essentializing those who are different. They may fetishize their authenticity, expecting them to be what Bell Hooks (1994) terms a 'native informant', who will provide easy access to the real lives of the oppressed. My study of women students and the curriculum provides a clear example of this process. The avowedly feminist module in American Studies taught at Expanding University had inadvertently created a trap for the only black student on the course. The focus on black women and their multiple struggles had positioned Adah, African daughter of a diplomat, with a privileged and cosmopolitan background, as a conduit to the lives of impoverished black women writers: 'They keep asking me how "do they cope", why do they think I know that?' (Adah). As Young indicates, it is difficult to negotiate such 'contradictions and tensions' and this can only be addressed by paying attention to detail over time; here, for example, by encouraging students to explore their own whiteness and its consequences, rather than homing in on the 'other'. The 'detemporalizing' mode of learning community, which suggests that the history of structural inequalities can be sidestepped, mitigates against such change processes.

## Strangers living in unoppressive cities

I want now to dwell a moment on Young's idea of the 'stranger'. It differs in interesting ways from Sara Ahmed's vision, where 'strangers are not simply those who are not known in this dwelling, but those who are in their very proximity *already recognised as not belonging*' (Ahmed 2000, p. 21, original emphasis). In contrast to Ahmed's conceptualization of the stranger, as one onto whom all fears and dangers are projected, and as personifying 'that which must be expelled from the purified space of the community' (ibid., p. 22), Young (op. cit.) sees strangers as benign figures. Rather than enforcing compliance and making others like themselves via a community embrace, they leave them free to be different and unviolated, while engaging in processes of mediation with them. It is only when we acknowledge that we are *all* strangers that we can begin to move forward to the unoppressive city. In my research with women students I discovered that far from being sucked into the homogenizing maw of the learning community, the different and the strange could be accommodated, so that the university might be an ideal site for Young's unoppressive city, rather than a learning community with shared values. This is not to say that the stranger/outsider discourse didn't operate; witness Adah who had this experience of student life:

> J. Q.: Did you experience any racism there?
> Adah: Yes, people would throw eggs at the window and they would draw little stick figures like Hangman on the path and once they wrote KK in chalk.

Yet amongst the women there was no unified view of what the university should be or do, rather multiple experiences of negotiating its difficulties and opportunities, facilitated by symbolic and imagined connections, as I shall discuss in the next chapter. According to Susan: 'When I walk through these gates I'm free', and when it worked, as it seemed to do for most of these women, it was a freedom to be unknown and untrammelled by the expectations of others.

Being a stranger might also be a deliberate strategy, especially for those who see university education as a part of life and not the be all and end all of it. Keeping a distance protected young black men who were studying for a degree in association with a community-based organization from giving too much of their valuable energies to the university community:

> When I was going to the university, I was y'know, in and out. I never really hung about there. I never really tried to socialize with anyone and that could be seen as a bad thing but in my case I've done all my socializing, I was there to do my work and do what I'd got to do for my future. I haven't got time to mess about.

> (Michael)

However, being a stranger is much more complicated for those right at the extreme of the learning spectrum. The homeless people understood that others saw them as uncomfortable strangers, 'figure(s) of the unknowable' (Ahmed, op. cit., p. 22) who were by no means desirably mysterious. In order to bring them into a learning environment, support workers had to abandon ideas of what was to be 'expected' from community members and instead be much more responsive. The ideal, pure and unified learning community was only a mirage, as this interview with Sam, a learning support worker for the homeless charity, demonstrates

> Sam: I was a mature student myself . . . I came straight out of that into this job with a kind of naive belief or naive desire to enable people to take the same route that I had taken which was essentially an access course and then university.
> JQ: So do you feel that background was important in enabling you to do this job?
> Sam: Yes, certainly on the sense of giving me a vision for it, even though that was a rather narrow view I feel, in the sense that I wanted everyone who came here to go on to university and to become professors. It was a very narrow, romantic vision that I have since had to expand on . . . I think what I try to do is find out what they are interested in and I try and fulfil that need if I can so that in that sense

I don't have to sell it because I am providing something that they want
. . . the notion of selling for me is about giving something to someone
that they don't necessarily want. They may need it, it may be useful
to them but it isn't something they are actively seeking at the time so
you have to sell it to them. Whereas people might actually be actively
seeking to do some music or do art and so those are the things I try
and push and concentrate on.

For the young people in jobs without training perhaps the problem is that
they are not strange enough. They are so familiar that they have become
invisible, noticed only when the service they provide is not satisfactory:

I love working in bars most, it's something probably I am better at than
anything . . . Well out of all the jobs I have been in the bar one is the one
I've done best . . . I always used to dread working on a bar . . . Well not
on a bar but working with customers. Because the public being what they
are . . .

(George)

They are perceived as non-, and probably never will be, belongers of university learning communities, so far outside that they can't even be a stranger
in the dwelling. None of those we interviewed talked about university at all;
for them this community on a hill did not exist.

## Learners' relations to learning communities and communities of practice

Here I seek to explore the impacts of learning communities and communities of practice further, drawing on my research data. This evidence suggests
that promoting 'learning community' as an idealized goal within formal
institutions does not seem to create belonging. For example, students who
had dropped out of university felt excluded and silenced within their institutions, despite the fact that all four universities in our study saw and presented
themselves as learning communities, as the Mission statement discussed

previously suggests. Universities did indeed have a plethora of initiatives which sought to draw in and support students. The typical range of support services included: mentoring schemes; a personal tutor scheme; work bank; onsite employment agency; careers service; chaplaincy; childcare; counselling; disability service; student health services; learning support; student information/guidance centre. In the accounts of student dropouts there were very few references to these pillars of the learning community. Indeed the learning community had very weak defences against the prevailing cultural narrative of working class dropout, which seemed to create a self-fulfilling prophecy that many such students would withdraw early:

> There's a well-trodden path from a lot of the schools sector into higher education. That can be seen almost as apathy. I think likewise there's this brick wall that has to be dismantled in terms of some of the other areas. If we don't do something to improve or reduce the dropout rates looking at all the human costs of all the mismatching, then it does filter down right down into the community where we're actually trying to convince people to come through. It does re-enforce those images of university as elitist. 'It costs too much to go to university', 'it's too hard to go to university', 'I couldn't possibly do the course' . . . I think it's a bit of an indictment that we're maybe failing to recognize and cope with those early signs of potential dropout.
>
> (Head of recruitment, research jury day)

In the jobs without training study, young people reflected on their experience of secondary schooling, which had left them feeling that they were very much positioned outside of any validated learning community and were unprotected by its espousal of community values:

> When I got to secondary school it all went downhill . . . it was just bullying and the teachers just chose to ignore us. The way I saw it in my experience is that they knew about the problem, they knew what was going on, they'd seen it happen and they did nothing about it.
>
> (Jo)

These were, overwhelmingly, young people who had not succeeded at school, and who did not buy into the self-image of the institution. They saw beneath the rhetoric and apparatus of the school learning community to the hierarchy that it masks: 'We were the thick bunch that got sent down to Connexions'. Ultimately they were extremely wary of re-entering into any kind of learning community:

> Interviewer: How about FE college?
> Jane: Pass.
> Interviewer: Could you go to college to do training?
> Tom: Not an option, no way.
> Interviewer: So you've been doing a cleaning job. Had you just taken this as a stop-gap?
> Liz: Yes, as you do, I did anything to occupy myself, anything apart from school.

They were aware that the ultimate purpose of the 'learning community' is self-perpetuation and that a whole plethora of bogus learning communities had been born of recent initiatives in the postcompulsory sector:

> I was doing the Customer Care thing one day a month [via Learning Agreement]. It was not like kosher it was like the whole place was set up for people who couldn't find jobs or had made themselves jobs, all the people who worked there were the sort of people who did.
>
> (Liz)

Notwithstanding these problems, the young people in our research valued some of the agents of learning communities with whom they had relationships. However, they were usually those who had gone far beyond the remit they had been assigned, or who broke the community mould. Some described how they had been helped informally by older adults, for others the Connexions service had been their only valuable source of personal advice and guidance:

My PA [personal advisor] basically has done a hell of a lot for me because he's helped me with all sorts . . . I deal with him all the time now because he knows all my background, he knows what I've done.

(John)

Coming here helped me out a lot . . . I was a little bit at a dead end, so I came here and they put me on the right tracks . . . They taught me to get over hurdles, look at other scenarios that are there which you can't always see. So I've gone different routes around things.

(Rick)

This was through Connexions, one person I ever had any success with there was Joe and I think it was because he was younger, you know like we were saying before. Because they understand what you're doing and he was great and he printed off all these apprenticeships for motor vehicles and stuff.

(Draco)

For others, Connexions was simply pushing a government agenda and failed to listen to the young people themselves: 'If you tell them one thing about you, that's the only thing you're about, and then you have to do something in that area' (Liz).

These young people seemed to need information, advice and guidance but one of the lessons of our research was that seeking to induct them into a fixed and formal notion of learning community will not and cannot work. Learning communities hold no magic or comfort for them and there is no common factor that will unify them, except perhaps the belief that: 'Because we've been out in the real world, we know more about what's going on' (Dick). As one PA concluded in her reflective diary:

Each young person is different, even though they are seen to be in a job with no training – he is happy with this and content with his life. This will make me more aware . . . so not to get caught up in the thought that they should move on to get a better job.

Across my research projects the closest thing to a learning community came in the voluntary sector organizations we explored in the learning brokerage project, the types of organizations now most threatened by lack of funding. Here it was not a question of being told and taught what was 'expected', but more of speaking out and learning: 'some young people will feel happier to do things if they are not obligated to do things, you're all on a level here you can work and do good things' (Leon, community arts project). The use of the term 'obligation' is interesting here, as learning communities usually favour a rhetoric of moral obligation, with codes of appropriate behaviour. Here in the community arts project, belonging is about working and doing 'good things' rather than being good. The emphasis shifts to what is being produced rather than the moral worth of the producer. The concept of communities of practice has more validity here, as do Lave and Wenger's (1991) ideas of 'situated learning', where learning takes place through everyday acts. Nevertheless, their idea of the 'way in', where the action shown by a master, followed by 'practice' where the learner does the act themselves, does not exactly capture the mutuality with which tutors and learners approach their work in this context:

> I think that the tutors actually part of their role is to pass on their skills at leading a group and that's what's the difference between here and other colleges . . . because with people all participating people eventually pick up the skills to lead and they can do that at any time in a group or workshop . . . and the boundaries are knocked down. And that's without being 'taught' there's no formulation for it you just pick it up.
>
> (Paul, tutor community arts organization)

For those learning more straightforward tasks, such as those that the young people in jobs without training had to do, communities of practice and situated learning is a reasonable descriptor of the process whereby they gain a sense of mastery and success that had previously eluded them:

> I've learnt as I've gone along and when I was working at the warehouse I was just like loading up the trolleys, taking out gear, getting the order

ready and bringing in stuff and they saw I was coping well and they offered me the job as the supervisor at night.

(Dave)

However, for the students who had dropped out, or those who had done badly at school, the overall ethos of mastery of practice is generally oppressive, rather than enabling, and the skills they are allowed to master will tend to fix rather than expand their horizons. First they are not convinced that they can ever master these practices: 'At first we all struggled, then the others seemed to get it so I didn't want to speak out' (computing student who had dropped out); second they are not convinced that mastery will ultimately lead to a desired goal:

> Student 'dropout': Out of seven engineers at college only two have
> remained engineers, the rest have gone into the Army, Navy or RAF.
> Some had apprenticeships then left them because they turned out to
> be dead ends.
> Interviewer: If you leave are there opportunities to get a decent job
> around here?
> Student 'dropout': Not really no. There are jobs. Good jobs very few . . .
> there are a lot of packing jobs but good jobs are scarce.

Failure to get to grips with the practices creates a sense of hopelessness and retreat amongst many homeless people:

> When we're talking about courses, basic skills things like that really put
> people off and it's about the age group which is usually white men aged
> about 25 to 35. A lot of people say to me, 'Oh I've done that already. I can't
> be bothered anymore'. It's almost like 'I've given up I don't want to do any
> more training because I did it before and I wasn't very good at it.'
>
> (Tania, homeless outreach worker)

Furthermore, these practices are not neutral, they are imbued with hegemonic values, particularly class values. They are tied to a normalized idea of a community member who talks and behaves in acceptable ways and who is expected to know certain things. For the young black men in London who were studying music at university, supported by the voluntary arts organization, when they were at university they were very clearly positioned outside the dominant community of practice:

> the way the tutors speak to us in a class, right, it's sometimes, it's not jargon, but because you haven't, um, maybe your upbringing, you just don't know about some sort of type of music . . . so when they're talking about some classical musicians it doesn't mean nothing to me. I can't relate to it . . . so if I would have done the assignments without the help I'm sure I would have failed.
>
> (Olly)

When it comes to those whose practices are not validated in any sphere and who must be trained to fit another more respectable mould, it seems that the communities of practice model breaks down completely. Homeless people, for example, are deemed to need basic skills, but seemingly without any idea of how they might apply them in practice. Their actual learning levels and competencies are disregarded:

> We can get money quite easily for basic skills classes and there's a need for it . . . we have got quite high illiteracy rates, we've also got high literacy rates as well simultaneously. There is money for basic skills and that is part of the government agenda. I felt very uncomfortable with some of the basic skills approach, some of it is good but a lot of it is judgemental, there's a sense of speaking properly and about writing properly and there's a lack of recognition of other skills because people acquire the skills they need for the life they are living. It seems to me most of our literacy skills are picked up not by doing literacy classes but by doing other types of work.
>
> (Sam, learning support worker homeless charity)

Providing learning in a vacuum is counterproductive. To become part of a community of practice requires some form of sanction and an identifiable goal and these sanctions and goals are socially circumscribed ones. As Sam astutely notes:

> Most people who are doing PhDs have learnt that language through actually having to read that sort of stuff and write that stuff. You just pick up the style as you go along. Whereas the Basic Skills agenda there isn't anything to achieve. There's no goal at the end to use it for.

What the communities of practice discussion tends to leave out, is how worthwhile those practices are to begin with, why some practices are targeted at some people and what values and privileges are assigned to them.

## Conclusion

In this chapter I have introduced the concepts of learning communities and communities of practice, taking a critical perspective on how such concepts create exclusions and idealizations that inhibit rather than promote learning. In opposition to the controlling reach of the community, I propose Iris Marion Young's idea of the 'unoppressive city' where people are allowed to mediate relationships as 'strangers', thus allowing rather than subduing difference (Young, op. cit.). In contrast to Ahmed's vision of the stranger as perceived threat (Ahmed, op. cit.), these strangers are comforting and inspiring in their willingness to be separate and also suggest new possibilities. In analyzing my research data I find that learning communities do very little for learners, except make them feel they can't belong. Similarly communities of practice form walls of self-protection and exclusion which leave others stranded outside.

Recently, interest has grown in the work of Ranciere and his concept of 'the division of the sensible' and its use for addressing 'inclusion' (see, for example, Žižek 2009). This argument, similar to Young's critique of 'community', is that for some to be 'included' depends on the perpetuation of the notion of exclusion of others and ultimately nothing can radically change. It could be said that learning communities and communities of practice are classic modes of 'inclusion' and as such ultimately retrogressive. Ranciere proposes instead 'emancipation' for all. This to me has echoes of distinctions once made between women's liberation and women's equality, as in the slogan: 'women who want to be equal to men lack imagination'. Liberation/emancipation depends on a new blueprint where what is possible, perceptible and palpable is redrawn. In the following chapter I will explore how it is the imagination and not the trappings of inclusion that best helps people learn to belong.

# Chapter 3

# Conceptualizing Imagined Social Capital

In this chapter, I will counterpose the concept of imagined social capital and symbolic community against those of learning communities and communities of practice that were discussed in the previous chapter. I will outline and explore the concept of imagined social capital (Quinn 2005a) and use it to interrogate a range of research data, and in doing so, will argue that imagined social capital is possibly our most potent resource for learning; much more powerful than learning communities or communities of practice. Here I take up Probyn's argument that 'different modes of belonging fold and twist the social fabric of life, so that we find ourselves in unexpected ways using desires for belonging as threads that lead us into unforeseen places and connections' (Probyn 1996, p. 22). This chapter follows such threads and how they are woven with others within symbolic and imagined networks. It privileges the imagined over the factual, recognizing the truth of Bachelard's dictum that 'we are never real historians, but always near poets' (Bachelard 1994, p. 6).

As discussed in the previous chapter, ideas of learning and community have been both quotidian and grandiose and encompass creating the perfect learning community across a whole institution or recognizing the minutiae of daily acts which go to build up a community of practice. It is not true to say that there are no symbols involved in this process. As I have discussed, the apparatus of a formal learning community positions itself via crude symbolization and there are myriad membership symbols of the community of practice. However, what I am interested in here are the ways in which learners create their own imagined and symbolic networks which cannot be predetermined or imposed.

I shall begin by discussing the notion of social capital, a concept which has been closely interwoven with educational aspirations to build learning communities. Bourdieu sees social capital as 'the aggregate of the actual or potential resources which are linked to the possession of a durable network of more or less institutionalised relationships of mutual acquaintance and recognition' (Bourdieu 1997, pp. 47–51). Membership of the group confers social capital but it has to be continually worked at. The nature of the social capital is shaped by the material, cultural and symbolic status of the group and its habitus or life world, and thus patterned by structural inequalities. Bourdieu has been enormously influential, not to say ubiquitous, in educational research. It could be argued that the thrust of his arguments have been misinterpreted, as implying a fixity to social capital; whereas change is built into his model of habitus: 'it is a dynamic concept, a rich interlacing of past and present, interiorised and permeating both body and psyche' (Reay 1997). However, his emphasis on 'durable' and 'institutionalised' relationships is one that I will challenge in my discussions of imagined social capital.

Policy makers prefer a more self-reliant strand of social capital theory, such as that found in Coleman (1990), Puttnam (2000) and Woolcock (1998). There are many discussions about the definitions of social capital. Dasgupta notes 'There is no single object called social capital, there is a multitude of bits that together can be called social capital. Each bit reflects a set of interpersonal connections' (Dasgupta 2002, p. 7). To provide a brief overview: Coleman sees 'bonding' social capital as the capital produced from linking with those with whom we are in close relationship and who share the same values, most notably family members. For Puttnam 'bridging' social capital refers to the trust and connections between people from different walks of life, which can be fostered by shared activities such as volunteering. Woolcock introduces the idea of 'linking' social capital, which is the ability to make connections with and gain resources from formal institutions, such as universities. Field (2003) summarizes a typology of social capital with these three different categories all associated with different forms of learning. In this typology there are relative degrees of relationships with formal learning environments, with linking social capital having the loosest relationship and seemingly the most 'open resources for identity change amongst adults' (ibid., p. 147).

Although this policy-favourable social capital is flavour of the month, there are many critiques. Feminists, for example, have argued that social capital theory, and popular arguments that our society lacks social capital and must build more, tend to neglect the unpaid and unacknowledged (usually female) labour that already underpins social networks: 'when we argue for the bonds of collectivities to be strengthened who do we think is already doing the bulk of the unpaid emotional and physical work' (Blaxter and Hughes 2000, p. 87). Others, such as Mayo, suggest that building more social capital for some inevitably reduces access to it for others. This may increase rather than reduce inequalities and thus social capital theory does nothing to address fundamental structural problems:

> Social policies to strengthen social capital may be compared with economic policies to extend the holding of share capital: particular individuals and groups may indeed benefit but the underlying structure of economic and social inequality remain relatively undisturbed. Particular individuals and groups may even come to experience increased social exclusion as a result.
>
> (Mayo 2000, p. 32)

The link between social capital theory and the promotion of learning communities is very strong. The purported function of learning communities is to build solid and sustainable networks that will foster the growth of social capital. This is tied to a policy goal to deliver compliant citizens who build social capital, not just for the good of themselves, but of the nation. Thus social capital is folded back into the whole. Social capital has been harnessed to an agenda of responsible citizenship and compliance.

## The birth of 'imagined social capital'

Discussions of social capital tend to be very literal ones and for this reason amongst others it has given me pleasure to intervene in the debate. I first developed the idea of 'imagined social capital' in 2005 and have since been asked to speak about it regularly and others have adopted it to their own uses too. Perhaps its appeal is that it does enter into the social capital debate full on but also attempts to subvert it. My argument is that imagined social capital is the benefit that is created by participating in imagined or symbolic networks These networks are much less tangible and measurable than the networks discussed in other branches of social capital theory, nevertheless as I shall demonstrate, can generate weighty forms of capital for those involved in them. The notion of imagined social capital was data driven; it emerged when I was trying to understand the ways in which the women university students I researched created belonging for themselves, in the face of what appeared to be curricular and pedagogical exclusion. The data generated by my research project seemed to point inexorably to forms of marginalization. As far as the curriculum was concerned, the lives and experiences of women seemed to play a marginal role, even where they were the majority of students. Pedagogically, men consistently garnished the most attention and the highest reward. In their home and work lives outside the university their caring for others and subordination in less powerful roles seemed to confirm Liz's statement that 'it's still a man's world'. When I explored these women's accounts of how they had negotiated and survived their complex educational and social lives, it was the symbolic and imagined networks that they drew upon, not any of the paraphernalia of the learning community. None of the mechanisms of learning community, such as student support or learning advice, featured in their accounts and there was little sense that they felt part of a community of practice. Instead they talked about how they had created symbolic and imagined networks and how these networks had supported and sustained them. As Bachelard argues: 'Mankind's nest, like his world, is never finished. And imagination helps us to continue it' (Bachelard, op. cit., p. 104).

Symbolic networks can be seen as networks with 'real' others that are created to perform a symbolic function. For example, a group of mature women students had christened themselves 'the ladies who lunch', re-inscribing their difference as something positive and supportive and also reclaiming a derogatory term. Imagined networks are those links created with unknown others who may even be mythical or fictional. For example, women talked about how they gained power from making imagined connections with 'really strong women' whom they did not know personally, but who they had read or learned about in their studies. It was the benefits created by these symbolic and imagined networks that enabled them to feel powerful enough to stay in the university, even when many forces were pushing them out. In promoting belonging and facilitating learning, imagined social capital, not 'community', was the key.

Most significantly, these were networks and benefits they created for themselves, not that were created for them. It is this element of creation and agency that is crucial. Here 'the imagined' is something different than, for example, 'the imaginary' presented in the work of Lacan, which appears, at least to this non-expert, to be highly deterministic. For Lacan it seems the imaginary is an inevitability and the roles of signifiers related to father, mother and baby in shaping that imaginary are inescapable. They can even be applied in a pseudo-mathematical formula (Lapping 2009). The drive is melancholia and a search for the lost object that can never be found. However, the object of desire that I am thinking about, as in the symbolic and imagined networks that learners create, can be found, can be summoned up and can be enjoyed and takes us forward rather than dragging us back:

> By the swiftness of its actions, the imagination separates us from the past as well as from reality; It faces the future. To the *function of reality*, wise in experience of the past . . . should be added a *function of unreality*, which is equally positive . . . If we cannot imagine we cannot foresee . . . Actual conditions are no longer determinant. With poetry, the imagination takes its place on the margin, exactly where the function of unreality comes to charm or to disturb – always to awaken – the sleeping being.
>
> (Bachelard, op. cit., pp. xxxiv–xv)

Although psychoanalytically infused writing, such as that of Deborah Britzman, can often be inspiring, psychoanalytic modes are, in my view, essentially conservative, in that they posit a set of universalizing patterns that we are literally born into. The concept of imagined social capital, on the other hand, is linked to resistance and re-envisioning. The strengths that it provides permit the possibility of transformation. For example, the women in my study partly created their imagined social capital through a shared sense of being survivors overcoming problems and struggles. In theory, imagined social capital might allow one to symbolically connect with father, mother *or* baby and explode the family drama.

## Totems of symbolic networks

It is interesting to think about how the women in my study built imagined social capital. Virgina Woolf argued that 'when a woman comes to write a novel she will find that she is perpetually wishing to alter the established values – to make serious what appears insignificant to man, and trivial what is to him important' (Woolf 1979, p. 49). The same appears to be true in the accounts women gave of their time in university, particularly in their diaries. One of the elements appears to be an investment in the symbolic nature of things which can act as emblems of belonging. My thinking on how diary data produced for the purposes of research might be interpreted has been influenced by the notion of 'leitmotifs' (Ribbens 1994). Leitmotifs are a recurring set of personal constructs, which appear to reveal the meanings that ideas and actions have for that person. In my interpretation they should not be seen as coming inherently from that person, but as having been accessed from culture. My own research diaries revealed such emblems of belonging too:

> *Another good day at the university explicitly because I did not retreat and withdraw from the experience . . . All these little things were big ones for me in staking a claim to be there and not just pretend to be. Felt strangely cheered by people admiring my boots.*
>
> *(J. Q., research diary)*

Truly little things mean a lot. The absolute centrality of kinky boots to my status of legitimacy and acceptance is not something easily understood by policy makers, but analysis is illuminating. The dynamic is of individual performance of identity and recognition and validation of that performance by members of the community, enabling one to be simultaneously different and the same. This seems less a question of transparently knowing and thus making a claim to possess, than a matter of taking pleasure in another's performance: what Young calls 'openness to unassimilated otherness' (Young, op. cit., p. 319). Similar processes were enacted repeatedly by my participants. Something more than learning is going on: a re-imaging of the self with and through others, without being absorbed or assimilated. Perhaps this might be a 'therapeutic sop' (Ecclestone 2004) if this re-imagined self were content to revel in its own performances, but there was agency and purpose in this process. Women were gathering strength to engage with both learning and life.

Using Iris Marion Young's idea of the unoppressive city, where strangers recognize each other and move on, I was able to understand that such moments of pleasure in the difference of others are constitutive of belonging, without expecting the other to become absorbed into a community of sameness. Returning to more recent entries in my research diary I can see this performance has now become a more conscious practice on my part, usually taking the form of (failed) admonitions to exhibit professorialism with a twist: *'wear rings, be light but firm'* (J. Q., research diary).

Clothes and their symbolic resonance are an interesting thread in the data I am exploring here. Beverley Skeggs (1997) made clear the connections between respectability and education, education being a prime means by which such respectability might be negotiated. In my research data, clothes were a significant marker of respectability, a first step that had to be mastered before education could be accessed:

I'm in a hostel right now but two to three weeks ago I still didn't look like this. I'm not the smartest person but a lot of people are a lot worse dressed than any of us here and that's another thing that puts you off going (to college) you just think 'I'm from the streets' . . . but whereas here they get into your minds 'look sort yourself', they get you into a hostel, they give you grants for clothes, they get you to present yourself better so you get more confidence, then they say well 'how do you feel about doing a course?'

(Cal)

Being homeless means negotiating how others see you. Certain forms of 'unsorted' appearance symbolize the streets and in order to have the confidence to return to study that street identification needs leaving behind. For the young people in jobs without training, job ambition also comes all rolled up in an outfit:

It's just not something I want to do no more, I want to go up a bit more than Sainsbury's [supermarket] . . . I want to get into something where I can wear suits and that . . . I want to become either a secretary or a receptionist.

(Chantelle)

Imagining the wearing of the suit has a powerful function. The suit is not a secondary aspect of the job, rather the job is the means whereby the suit can be worn and with it the symbolic power of the network of respectable workers can be accessed. These totems of symbolic networks are not trifles but important signifiers of imagined social capital.

## What I am not

Although the women students in my higher education study were a heterogeneous group, including mature students and working class women, they were, by virtue of their position as students, privileged learners, with the luxury of a university education. The subjects they studied offered opportunities to expand their connections with symbolic others and the culture of the university offered possibilities to meet and open up to strangers, as discussed in Chapter 2. They may thus be in the most likely place for imagined social capital to develop. I was very interested to see whether imagined social capital had any validity when applied to a disadvantaged and marginalized group of people and so moved to use the concept to interrogate data from young people in jobs without training. I discovered that they did create and avow their belonging to certain symbolic networks such as those who 'knew about life' or who 'learned from doing not from books'. However, it seemed that imagined social capital functioned mainly as a benefit they gained from identifying 'what I am not', in positioning themselves apart. They gained strength from envisioning networks of those who were truly desperate – such as those heavily addicted to drugs, and asserting that this would never be them:

> Liz: Exmouth is full of it like cocaine and stuff.
> Interviewer: So it's easy to get into that then?
> Liz: Yes you hear about it all the time.
> Interviewer: What would stop you from going down that route do you think?
> Liz: I've got a lot of friends who've gone that way and just to see them now and think 'Oh God' disgusting. They're just, and any money they get goes straight away on drugs.
>
> (Liz)

They also repudiated the networks of their compliant peers who had continued from school into college: unlike their friends they were not hamsters on a training wheel, trapped in cycles of college courses that they didn't want: '. . . so they've all finished their courses and realized they don't want to do it so they are doing more courses . . . Pointless isn't it?' (Fred).

Creating these images of negative symbolic networks helped to validate their own decisions, to choose work and to take it seriously. This created a form of imagined social capital, a resource that made them feel more powerful and increased their confidence in themselves. However, as Bourdieu argues, social capital is only meaningful when it is legitimated. The imagined social capital generated by the women students had enabled them to do their degrees and thus become equipped with a legitimated resource with some cultural and economic power. For the young people in jobs without training, there was no legitimation of their position as people who preferred low-skilled work to study, and their imagined social capital could not be turned very easily into material reward. As I shall discuss, imagined social capital is a situated resource, with different meanings and modes of operation in different contexts. Using the concept across my different research studies I have been able to develop a nuanced exploration and will continue this in the remainder of this chapter.

## Imagined social capital and the natural world

A sustained relationship to the natural world in south west England (the world of the seagulls and rivers in Alice Oswald's monumental poem: 'Dart' (2002)), was an interesting dimension of the study with young people in jobs without training. Many of these young people lived in rural areas or by the sea and the specificities of this often ignored rural context appeared to generate certain forms of imagined social capital connected to the natural world. There was limited celebration of the pastoral, and rather more complaints about the restrictions of living in the countryside: 'Oh yes a lot of tourists come down here, but it's not very busy the rest of the time . . . they always try to get some extra staff then they're dismissed as soon as summer's over' (Jo)

Yet the natural world did weave throughout the accounts in interesting ways. Animals, for example, often surfaced, whether it was farm animals like pigs and cows: 'I love my job it's really varied and I like being outside, it's practical and every day is different. I like the animals too' (Ben); or horses that they enjoyed riding and caring for:

Becky:  It's what I've always wanted to do, look after horses.
Interviewer:  Where do you see yourself in five years' time?
Becky:  I think I would like to be an RSPA inspector.

Or animals that they liked to hunt: 'I am going beating a few times a week' (Jane);

'I kept myself to myself . . . I had to walk away from trouble because I've got a shotgun license and I don't want to lose it' (John).

Being 'outside' in the fields or on water was important too, whether at work or at play: 'I don't know they (school) kept on and on and harping at me. I didn't want to be at school. I wanted to be at home at the farm outside'; 'I'm out every night teaching canoeing with the cadets'; 'I never want to be stuck inside in an office'; 'I would hate to be stuck in this four-walled environment day in day out'. These connections represented freedom, pleasure and opportunity to be happy in the body and also locations where they might display expertise. So, they gain imagined capital from symbolic connections with the non-human that simply did not figure in any of the other studies I am discussing. Whether this could be called 'social' capital is a good question. Possibly it remains social because the networks are with others who have similar beneficial relationships to the non-human. This is the symbolic network, not of nature lovers but of nature familiars.

This links to ideas developed by the *convivium* on 'Passionate Natures' held in Cambridge in 2007 and which I noted at the time in my research diary. Some of the questions that the *convivium* explored were as follows:

> How does nature help us think? Why do certain places posses or enable types of experience and forms of wisdom that are unavailable elsewhere? Might thoughts, as well as species therefore, require particular environments with which to exist – and can thoughts be considered indigenous to particular landscapes? . . . We wanted to know how emotional attachments to the natural world could be valued and how such attachments are shaped by, and can shape culture.
>
> (Mellor 2007, pp. 18–19)

If we take these questions in relation to the accounts of the young people, then possibly the places they inhabit encourage a form of embodied thinking which is pragmatic and self-sufficient, not extravagant and expansive. Nature is an everyday reality for them, not an idealized picture, and generates a grounded wisdom, which is as much about limits as it is about opportunities. Theirs is not a romantic sensibility at all and neither do they express themselves rhetorically. In the wider domain these symbolic attachments to nature are valued by them, but quite invisible to others, or if they are acknowledged, they are seen as signs of a retrograde 'peasant' sensibility. These networks may sustain them in everyday living but they do not offer much to bargain with in the world of employment, skills and training. Indeed the drive in the UK, encapsulated in the Leitch Review of Skills (Leitch 2006), is to push them back from the outside into classrooms and training centres until they are 18. The role of education is to 'civilize' them and subdue the natural.

In contemporary educational research there seems limited attention to the natural world, although we could argue this has not always been the case, as the classic work of Rousseau is also about subduing nature. Although there is a growing literature on how to teach and encourage sustainability, this is not sufficient to address the deeper issues raised by the cultural debate on nature and epistemology. The philosophical questions about thought and place raised in the Passionate Natures *convivium* were not only relevant to the young people in my study, but also to myself. The linking of thought and place was a live issue for me, writing this book mainly at home in rural Devon, a very different location from the dismal Lancashire town where I wrote my first book:

> *'Relate to my drawing on the natural world sitting at this window looking at water. How different will this book be than the one produced over the alley in Darwen?'*
>
> *(J. Q., research diary)*

Did watching geese, ducks, oystercatchers and egrets encourage 'lines of flight' and thoughts that skipped or skimmed? Like the birds of Alice Oswald (op. cit.), flying down the rivers and sea of the south-west where: 'There one dreamed bare clothed only in his wings': was there freedom to think elementally? Certainly my relation to the natural world was not the same as the young people in the study, in that I could not take it for granted, it constantly surprised and delighted me. Perhaps it did facilitate thinking about, and with, pleasure and joy. Jeremy Mynott (2009), in his recent book *Birdscapes: Birds in our Imagination and Experience,* has argued that 'birds are good to think with' in encouraging a metaphorical way of understanding abstract things, and it is true that this metaphorical cast has become a feature of my recent work. There is a darker side of course. As a privileged incomer to the south-west I was amongst those driving up house prices and making it more difficult for such young people to stay where they were born. It would take them a very long time of hard work to make what I could earn in a short time watching birds. Engaged in sentimental relations with birds and animals I was a threat to their traditions. Moreover, I tended to create their everyday activities as picturesque, marvelling that they were so different from those of my own suburban/urban youth on Merseyside.

This discussion reveals that imagined social capital, like other forms of social capital, is only of benefit when it is legitimated. Imagined social capital cannot fly free of forms of privilege and inequality and structures of educational provision. Universities may offer opportunities for women as students and as workers to cash in their imagined social capital for the future and become like me, a self-indulgent professor and birdwatcher, but post-16 training beckons young people back into a world of failure that does not validate their symbolic sense of self. Our aim should be an education system that permits a harmony between the symbolic and the material worlds of learners, and I shall return to this issue in Chapter 5.

## Imagined social capital and nostalgia and memory

Moving on to locate and explore imagined social capital in relation to those students in the university dropout study, a different emphasis emerges. Here imagined social capital was a product of what Hirsch and Smith call 'the politics of nostalgia', where nostalgia perpetuates 'a necessary engagement with the past and an act of witnessing in the present' (Hirsch and Smith 2002, p. 9). The students in this study all lived and studied in provincial areas which had once revolved around traditional industries, now declined and disappeared. The symbolic networks that they attached themselves to tended to be the 'lost' working communities of their localities: the tightly knit enclaves of pottery or mining. Only the vestiges of these communities actually remained, such as the satisfyingly shaped kilns dotted across the Potteries, yet in family memory these communities were very much present:

> I live on a council estate . . . people from that kind of place think educa-
> tion isn't important and you're getting that drummed into you all the
> time. They say you don't need to get an education, get a job, go into an
> industry, but industry is very low now in this area.

As discussed in Chapter 1, in many ways their narratives, rather than being a personal story of the authentic or inescapable self, were acts of witness: 'an act of retelling or, in the language of performance, of 'twice-behaved behaviour" (ibid., p. 9) where communal stories of the past were re-circulated.

There were different local trends shaping these symbolic networks. For example, in Scotland language and dialect was a marker of the symbolic community, much more strongly than in other areas. In the Scottish research jury day the idea was raised that in dropping out, students were reasserting their own language and resisting the fake language of the university. This was linked to what seemed a strong local culture of pride and resistance. In Wales, visions of different landscapes, different valleys and how they used to be shaped by industry had a powerful symbolic weight. In the research jury day here they discussed the separateness of each valley, the minutely localized culture that meant moving from one to another was not a part of local history.

The example of the dropout study demonstrates that imagined social capital might be a problematic resource. It is a source of strength, enabling them to think – I come from a place with strong traditions. It is possible to work and live with others in common purpose. However it may be a trap as well, leading to mournful conclusions – nothing will ever replace this lost community; education is a useless compensation. Whenever these students made a move, the symbolic resonance of the past seemed to follow them, shaping their decisions and how they felt about them. Ersatz symbolic networks, such as recasting certain areas as cultural quarters and heritage sites, did not do much to respond to the loss of the daily culture of purposeful work. Memory is a living and not a dead thing: 'Far from being the reliquary or trash can of the past, it sustains itself by believing in the existence of possibilities and by vigilantly awaiting them, constantly on the watch for their appearance' (de Certeau 1984, p. 87).

By means of the politics of nostalgia, imagined social capital created challenges to universities to compensate for these lost communities and to deliver learning with some of the qualities that had been exhibited by them. Universities need to take these memories seriously and work with them in a respectful way.

## Imagined social capital and abjection

In thinking about the power of symbolic networks, I wondered about the crushing symbolic pain, as well as loneliness, of those who had no networks at all. During this time I noted in my research diary a TV documentary called *See Me Disappear*, which told the stories of two people who had lain dead for months, even a year, with no one knowing and no one attending their funeral. Simultaneously, in my life I was the only family member who attended my own aunt's funeral: a woman with a tragic history who had lived in institutions for many years. The other mourners were two hospital visitors. These traumatizing incidents summoned thoughts of Kristeva's abject:

> The corpse seen without God and outside of science, is the utmost of abjection. It is death infecting life. Abject. It is something rejected from which one does not part, from which one does not protect oneself as from an object. Imaginary uncanniness and real threat, it beckons to us and ends up engulfing us.
>
> (Kristeva 1982, p. 4)

While the corpse is the ultimate abject object, other things are included in the category such as refuse and bodily fluids:

> refuse and corpses show me what I permanently thrust aside in order to

live, These body fluids, this defilement, this shit are what life withstands, hardly and with difficulty on the point of death.

(ibid., p. 3)

What are the relationships between abjection and the negative power of zero imagined social capital, and where does learning fit in? This thinking led me to re-explore the data with homeless people. Of all those I had researched, they appeared closest to abjection – were in a state of being cast out from homes, jobs, previous lives and they were also configured by others as 'scum' and 'dirt' and described their lives as 'shit'. Their bodies were often in a state of decay, and, indeed, the manager of the homeless organization talked to us in detail, and with some horror, about ulcers, gangrene and unbearable smells, which he combated with incense. He grieved the high rate of early death amongst the homeless people he worked with. The corpse was literally a step away.

Unsurprisingly, a complex picture emerges of how the homeless people managed their abjection, which they were more conscious of than anybody else could be. They perceived themselves as excluded: 'what is abject . . . the jettisoned object is radically excluded and draws me toward the place where meaning collapses' (ibid., p. 2). As Alan said: 'when you're homeless you feel very isolated and you feel the whole world is against you especially if you are in big cities and you don't know anybody'. Their entering into learning opportunities seemed partly fuelled by a fear of disappearing. They created imagined social capital as a means of manoeuvring themselves out of the abject category and constituting themselves away from the border. Learning appeared to be the most useful tool for this. For example, they took up symbolic links with worthy positionings, such as 'social worker', as a way of imagining themselves as different. Learning opportunities that made these symbols possibilities were the key to them creating and building imagined social capital.

> . . . when I was on drugs the only thing I thought about was getting up
> and getting a score, making my money and getting a score every day . . .
> One day I just woke up and thought 'fuck this I've had enough'. It isn't

a life it's an existence. That's why I want to be a social worker because I've been there . . . *If I can just stop one other person going down that road then that's me happy.*

(Cal, my italics)

In saying this last sentence Cal's tone became sententious, even sanctimonious, as if he had momentarily inhabited the body of this mythical virtuous social worker.

Similarly, Alan, in the following exchange, as a way of managing his current behaviour, imagines himself in the future almost as the kind of textbook reformed alcoholic of the type often found in a soap opera:

I would still say I have a drink problem but *until the day comes when I can say I'm giving up for me* . . . the thing is because it's not within me to give up and change my way of life yet . . . I can go weeks without having a drink but the problem is I start to get bored.

(Alan, my italics)

It is important to recognize that they are speaking in this way not because they are essentially different as homeless people, but as a way of managing the attributions placed on homelessness.

The fact that the workers in the learning centre can envision them as something other than abject is a powerful pull which has made a substantial difference to their lives and prospects:

JQ:  What would you do if there was no learning centre?

Cal:  I'd still be here, but I wouldn't be going to college more than likely I wouldn't have the volunteering job . . . I wouldn't have all those skills I've got on the computer. This place, the workers in the learning centre have done more for me in the last four months than what probation have in two years.

Pete:  Probation aren't really interested; all they are doing is making sure you stay out of trouble and if your face doesn't fit and they don't like you then all they want you to do is fail. Any excuse and they'll put

you back to court whereas here if you're genuine and you really want
to help yourself they'll help you.

JQ: Do you feel that you don't have to explain yourself here?

Alan: No you don't. (all nodding)

(focus group discussion)

To Kristeva, encountering the abject is a reflex action, a gagging at something out of place that forces itself on us, like the skin on hot milk: 'The
repugnance, the retching that thrusts me to the side and turns me away from
defilement' (ibid., p. 2). Yet it is also a form of judgement about what is out
of place. For the learning support workers, effective working with homeless
people required a conscious suspension of judgement, a refusal to position
them as abject. This was a pedagogical position and not just a personal
choice: 'It's also about that blame thing and I don't want to blame anyone.
I don't want to begin from that judgemental point of view and I don't want
to be someone who's going out to cure this problem' (Sam, learning support
worker). Learning can happen when everyone allows symbolic networks and
imagined social capital to be a possibility, and not just a ridiculous fantasy,
and also where capabilities to enter the symbolic network are recognized.

## Conclusion

In this chapter I have outlined and developed my theory of imagined
social capital and demonstrated why I think that this is more important for
learners than the mechanisms of learning communities and communities
of practice. I explain how I have added to existing theorizations of social
capital by formulating imagined social capital as the benefits that accrue
from symbolic or imagined networks. Symbolic networks may be networks
of those we know who are given a symbolic function, imagined networks
may be with those we don't know personally, or who may not even exist, but
with whom we can imagined desired connections. These networks provide
resources of power and resistance and appear to be more useful for survival
than formalized support networks are, although their potential to produce

change depends on how far they are legitimized. These are networks learners create for themselves rather than those that are created for them or that they are deemed to be born into. They are partly constructed via totems, such as dress, as I discuss. I explore imagined social capital as a localized and situated phenomenon that takes different shapes. Looking across my studies I demonstrate how it is created in relation to the natural world, nostalgia and memory and abjection and what the positive consequences may be for learners when educators take imagined social capital seriously.

# Chapter 4

# Re-imagining Educational Spaces

In this chapter, I will consider how we might re-imagine belonging, in both home and educational spaces. I will discuss how learners cross and recross the bridges between them, taking up themes of alienation and searching in the processes of learning to belong. The bridge is a potent image of suspension:

> the bridge is ambiguous everywhere; it alternately welds together and opposes insularities. It distinguishes them and threatens them. It liberates them from enclosure and destroys autonomy . . . But at the same time as it offers the possibility of a bewildering exteriority, it allows or causes the re-emergence beyond the frontiers of the alien element that was controlled in the interior . . . so that in recrossing the bridge and coming back within the enclosure the traveller henceforth finds there the exteriority that he had first sought by going outside and then fled by returning. Within the frontiers, the alien is already there!
>
> (de Certeau 1984, pp. 128–9)

The poet Ann McKay uses this image of crossing the bridge to and from home to enact the drama of interior/exterior and escape/alienation. 'Anubis on the Craigavon Bridge' sees the narrator, both God and dog, desperately, but fearfully, 'crawling along the white line' on the bridge across the river to 'Home', impelled to make the journey, but doing so as slowly and painfully as possible.

In exploring ambiguities and the difficulties of the crossing and recrossing of bridges, theories of space have proven the most useful tools. Educationalists are drawing increasingly on spatial concepts to understand the changing nature of education. In my own work on higher education, as I discuss in

Chapters 2 and 3, I have used them to understand how students construct their own vision of universities as 'protected spaces' and to reconceptualize universities as potentially more akin to 'unoppressive cities' than to learning communities. Noyes (2004) has demonstrated that the notion of learning landscapes is a useful educational research tool. He illustrates that, as a metaphor, landscape can 'enable education thinkers to conceptualize the complex framework of sociocultural influences that shape the learner using prior knowledge of their own environment' (Noyes 2004, p. 39). In doing so, he focuses on four constituent elements: climate, geology, human intervention and time, which influence the learner (in his case, of mathematics at a time of transfer to secondary school) and argues for use of the landscape metaphor in other educational contexts. However, I would argue that the notion of landscape can, and has, been extended in significant ways that are not so earth-bound, to show that: 'landscape is a form of representation and not an empirical object' (Rose 1993, p. 88). It is this more cultural understanding of space that I have found most evocative and useful.

Spatial theorists working in the fields of social and cultural theory have demonstrated how we occupy multiple landscapes simultaneously: fragmented and multi-layered, existing in different dimensions including those of the senses and the imagination. These are 'geographies of the possible' (de Certeau, op. cit.), not rational nor confined to actual places, but suffused with thoughts and feelings: 'a geography of memory as much felt in the body as seen' (Tonkiss 2000, p. 2). Pile and Thrift's *City A–Z* is one text which tries to map such multiple landscapes or indeed cityscapes. Theirs is 'not so much an overview as an "underview" of the confusion and profusion of the city . . . they are territories in which every place is always a junction on the way to somewhere else' (Pile and Thrift 2000, p. xiv). Having already envisaged the university in city terms myself, I find their mapping of diverse geographies of the possible potentially creative. Cultural geography helps us to see that the real and the shadow actually merge, that all space is part fantasy, including educational institutions. This chapter will begin by exploring ways in which learners construct home and belonging and how this relates to their experiencing of educational institutions. Then it will try to re-imagine educational spaces in two ways. First it will seek to recognize those multiple spaces where learning can take place in unrecognized and non-validated forms. Second, it will seek to re-imagine formal educational spaces, such as universities, schools and colleges.

## House or home?

Notions of belonging are intrinsically bound up with thoughts of home. This is an inevitable relationship, as 'all really inhabited space bears the essence of the notion of home' (Bachelard 1994, p. 5). Educational spaces consciously try to reproduce some of the shelters of home, from the home corner in nurseries, to the 'family' atmosphere of universities. However, this ersatz home never quite works, nor does it countermand the regulatory nature of these spaces. 'Home' cannot be simply reproduced because it is a state of mind, a symbolic space both painful and joyful. 'Home is so sad' as Philip Larkin says, both to be in and to lose. Nevertheless, powerful symbolic relationships between educational spaces and home are generated by students themselves. In my study of women students I found that dominant perceptions of what home meant were transversed. Rather than affirming that '. . . the house shelters daydreaming, the house protects the dreamer, the house allows one to dream in peace' (ibid., p. 6), for these women, it was the public space of the university that had that function. The university was the space of dreams, while the 'house' was a place of threat to body and mind, where they were subject to violence from partners, or could not think because of the demands of family life. In her diary, Susan, who found freedom in the university, constantly refereed to her home as 'the house', using home only in an institutionalized sense, as in the note accompanying her research diary: 'Bye for now from the Home for the Terminally Stressed'. She configured her home as a place of entrapment, where 'You get stretched so thin it makes a hole and you disappear into it'. The bounds were her own sense of duty to her children and parents and she manipulated and deployed various resonant cultural narratives about imprisonment and escape, applying them to the home and the university. This was taken up with alacrity (and hilarity) by the rest of her focus group:

Susan: 'My daughter's 14 and I think just four more years until I come
to the end of my sentence.'

Grace: 'Yes 18 years, if you'd murdered someone you would have got
less time!'

Susan: 'Yes I'd be out on remission by now.'

Joanne: 'You could have done your degree in prison!' (lots of laughter)
(focus group, American Studies, Pleasant College)

However, this home/house relationship may be seen as particularly aged,
gendered and also raced. Patrick, a young black man with no family respon-
sibilities, studying a music degree via community arts, positioned it in a very
different way:

I think that the times you go to university in the time away from home is
like, it cuts your hand off 'cause when you're over in university you've got
to pay for your way over there, you're away from home and then when
you've done that you have to come back home and try to fit into everything
and you haven't got no money and that wasn't realistic to me.

For Patrick the university is a site of mutilation, not escape, because it is at
home that he is free to pursue his creative life and university simply gets in
the way, cutting off his music-making hand. An equally arresting image to
Patrick's severed hand comes in this exchange with Cal, a homeless learner
who had been offered the possibility of becoming a student at a specialist
residential college:

JQ: What did you think of the tutors at the residential college?

Cal: Wow, I didn't want to leave that at all, I wanted to nail myself down
to the floor.

Only such drastic measures, it seemed, would help him feel secure that
this haven would be a reality for him, a young man for whom the house
he had left behind in Yorkshire was nothing but 'shit', as I shall discuss. As
de Certeau confirms, people make spaces by their uses of them: 'space is

a practised place . . . the street geometrically defined by urban planning is transformed into a space by walkers' (de Certeau, op. cit., p. 117) and they reconfigure those spaces in different ways and with different purposes.

When talking about home one inevitably moves to thinking about family relationships. Family and education have become difficult to tell apart so that part of being constituted as a desirable family is the condition of being educated, and part of the condition of being educated is having a desirable family. For educationalists, this idealized sense of the family has become embedded and naturalized. The rhetoric of family values is often espoused, and even exaggerated. However, the close mutuality of family relations is not actually practiced in most formal settings and only in the community arts organizations did the reciprocity of family life have much daily reality:

> The whole thing in the uni was that it wasn't like a family network . . . but that's how uni's supposed to be, the tutors are not really meant to be in it with you, like engaged in any way because there's a big class or whatever . . . over here there's more of a friendly atmosphere.
>
> (Patrick, community arts organization)

## This is your home town

'Home', too, extends beyond the family space, to embrace home towns and home countries. I sought to trace images of home across all my participants' accounts, and how their imagining of what home was linked to their learning. As with the women students, they all needed to imagine educational spaces as spheres of protection. For those for whom formal learning spaces had proved dangerous and threatening, such as many of the young people in jobs without training, and some of those who had dropped out of higher education, these spheres of protection and senses of being at home with learning were often found in informal contexts, as I shall discuss further later.

The motif of the provincial home town, a place of strong emotional ties but also a carrier of shame and stigma, was extremely strong in the research with students who had dropped out of university. The significance of the home town in shaping opportunities for learning cannot be underestimated. For these ex-students, who had mostly gone to university locally, and often stayed living at home, there was a pervasive cultural narrative of provincial second class citizenship. As the chair of one research jury day concluded, the towns in our study were all 'gloomy areas with lots of social problems':

> I think it's part of the perception of a failing area with things like being labelled the worst city.
>
> (student 'dropout', England)

> Well it's a working class area, it has old steelworks and everything and for more and more people the jobs have disappeared . . . so you've got a lot of like where do we go from here you know because there's no jobs so we might as well go on benefit really.
>
> (student 'dropout', Wales)

> Interviewer: Can you give me a word that sums up your town?
> Ex-Student: Boring.
>
> (student 'dropout', Northern Ireland)

> Now the streets are dead. The town centre is not the best especially at night. It has got a lot of little dark alleys and dark streets. Lots of fights at the taxi rank on Friday nights.
>
> (student 'dropout', Scotland)

Although the prevailing whiteness of these areas and students allowed them the privileges and the problems of positioning themselves as the 'norm', they also perceived that they lacked the energy and cultural capital of more cosmopolitan and multi-cultural contexts. They internalized the torpor of their home surroundings: 'People from London and from other places they were more fun and more experimental and more just went for it – like had more balls'. As dropouts they were positioned as actually adding to the decline of the local area: 'Dropout has a knock on effect. It spreads disaffection across the community in small pockets' (adviser, Student Services).

They could feel they were doing their bit to make their home town even more depressing to live in.

While they were extremely loyal to home and the familiar, this came with a sense of resignation. The university itself created feelings of not being at home even in their own home towns: 'the people who lived in halls were part of the environment, whereas I felt like a bit of an outsider, even though I lived around here and it was my town.' As I have argued (Quinn 2004a), they had become positioned in a cultural narrative that accepts that working class students will go to university, but suggests that this will always be a flawed experience with a propensity to failure. However, to see the ties of home as punitive would be to miss the point. Their belonging at home was a process of mutuality and reciprocity where they worked with the other members of their family for the common good (see Thomas and Quinn 2007, for a full discussion). We need to move beyond accounts of what these learners lack, to see the strengths they bring to their university study.

For those young people in the jobs without training study, the parameters of home were even more circumscribed. Their interviews circled their streets and neighbourhoods, marking out the limits of where they would or could go: 'they are all drug dealers down there – horrible' (Tamara), and the close networks working for or against them: 'someone stole my bike, but they didn't know who I know . . .' (John).

Opportunities for what seemed like escape were rejected or evaded:

Adam: I was offered training in London but said no because I don't want to go to London.
Interviewer: Do you still want to stay in Ciren?
Dick: Yeah, yeah well I do at the moment actually, well I've got a girlfriend.
Interviewer: Because when we talked before you were really keen to get away from here?
Dick: Yeah but now she's pregnant she wants to stay by her family and that.

The rural locations they lived in and the lack of transport and social housing meant that opportunities to move away from home or get a new job were limited: 'I've got to figure out a way how to get there [a new job] by 8.30 am tomorrow and there's no trains or buses that go directly there' (Liz). However, although the home-neighbourhood was circumscribed, it worked – it was the place that provided links to the job world – not Connexions or Jobs Centre Plus: 'My mum is my boss at Asda', 'I stepped into my cousin's shoes', 'I'm going to work for my uncle'. Although home could be volatile, it was a place where the terms of engagement were understood, unlike school or college. The accounts that the young people give of their secondary schooling is of faceless institutions where bullying and hostility shaped the daily life: 'I never used to enjoy school. I used to get picked on all the time . . . I used to go and see a counsellor at school but I just didn't have, I couldn't talk to anyone.' Education left them confused and insecure: 'Give me a book and I can't understand it.' School was literally dangerous and so leaving school generally signalled a retreat from education into the home, with only three people in our study even considering returning to study at college:

> They didn't want no trainees. You just go in, you train as you do the job. I thought that sounded good. I like doing that sort of work because studying I never got the hang of, cause textbooks and that, it doesn't really register in my brain that much.
>
> (George)

> I have thought about it [college], but when I look after the kids from college on day release [at the farm where he was working] I realize I'm in the best position as I'm learning more and more each day and I don't need a classroom to learn it.
>
> (Ritchie)

## Homeless learning

What about those people who don't have the luxury to be ambivalent about their home, because they do not even have one? 'The homeless' are a group defined by their lack, yet 'home' is a set of values which this group of people did not necessarily espouse. In their accounts, home was a place to escape from or a place that they had blown apart by self-destructive behaviour. In their current lives they were always engaged in protecting self and space in a very direct way. Their life was a running battle across territories with no opportunity to retreat and reflect. They made an interesting distinction between 'marking your place' and being confident, with confidence being linked to education:

> JQ: You are all confident aren't you or talk like you are?
> Cal: To be honest with you living on the streets being in hostels, you've got to be able to stand up for yourself, you've got to be forwards . . . I don't mean so you go in as Mr Hard Man or be obnoxious . . . Since I've been coming here . . . my confidence has grown a lot . . . because you're educating yourself.
>
> (Cal, focus group, homeless charity)

Home and learning is supposed to be the apogee of civilized life – buy a house, get qualified, get a good job. Although on one level this has been challenged by the recession, there are also many indicators of retreat into the home, to avoid the costs and problems of engaging with the world outside. Home is supposed to provide security, but it is also characterized by boundaries and stasis. For the homeless people this may be exactly what they don't want:

> Maybe some people's lifestyles may be adopted in that some people might prefer to live in hostels, to move from place to place because the other lifestyle is about getting a job, going to work at 9 o'clock every day and yes OK you've got money for cars, money for holidays, but those things aren't particularly attractive to them so they think this is a lifestyle I'm happy with.
>
> (Sam, learning support worker, homeless charity)

. . . they are a very mobile community, moving around from location to location, institution to institution. But also they don't engage because the whole idea of education is seen as a stick to beat people with.

(Tania, outreach worker, homeless organization)

Despite this negative attitude to home, comfort, security and learning could be experienced as interlinked in a highly embodied way, where learning opens up the possibility of belonging, in a way a mere house could never do:

JQ: Have you seen any changes in people when they have started to get involved?

Tom: Yes you can see people get excited by what they're doing and kind of rejuvenated. Getting out of the rain for an hour and coming in here and accessing the internet listening to music or just playing games even, it can be quite a breath of fresh air for people I find and you can physically see it in people they come in, they're a lot more chilled out, a bit more at peace with themselves . . . a lot of the people we work with don't have anywhere else, they don't have any other comfort zone that they can get to if they need to.

(Tom, support worker, homeless organization)

## Mothers and not being at home in the world

Talking about belonging and home generates a further dimension and introduces its shadow side: the uncanny. As de Certeau suggests: 'There is no place that is not haunted by many different spirits hidden there in silence, spirits one can "invoke" or not. Haunted places are the only ones people can live in' (de Certeau, op. cit., p. 108). Schostack and Schostack discuss the significance of the uncanny in the following terms:

The inside is haunted by an outside as when at the edge of consciousness the shadows at night make shapes which may be glimpsed only when looking awry (Žižek 1991). It is when being at home there is a sense of unfamiliarity, a sense of the uncanny (Royle 2003), that is not feeling at home in the world. It is this disjunction between a world that is 'our home' and a world that is somehow beyond it and threatens its unity, its order, its sense of safety.

(Schostack and Schostack 2006, p. 8)

It seems perhaps obscure to link the uncanny with learning to belong, but there were certainly uncanny elements in my studies. Reading Sarah Waters's novel *The Little Stranger* helped to draw my attention to mothers as a conduit to this world beyond: 'What is it mother? Why are you looking? What can you see?' (Waters 2009, p. 308). It reminded me of the mother/daughter relationships in my research with women students. In this study mothers were uncanny presences who always seemed to slip in uninvited and to be present just out of eyesight. It was not part of my research plan to explore mother/daughter relationships, or mothers' experiences of education, but in interviews and diaries particularly, talk of education led to mothers, especially the opportunities they had lost or foregone. Those mothers who were dead seemed to exert the most powerful influence of all:

> Grace: As I say I was always quiet, a '*good girl*' (deep voice) I was
> youngest I was quite solitary I was with my mother . . . (sighs) oh dear.
> J. Q. (playfully): So are you bad girl now you are a student?
> Grace (looking very uncomfortable): Oh no, not bad, not bad, I don't
> think so.

(Grace, 62)

There was a close association between learning and relationships with mothers, and this, I have argued (Quinn 2004b), is because mother and child negotiate reality: what can be known, what is real and what is imagined, regularly crossing and recrossing the boundaries between them. They are engaged in a mutual knowledge project, in which the terms are floating and the door to the uncanny is left ajar. This state of liminality may be hard work, but it is also potentially full of fantastic pleasures; as I can testify from my own forays into the uncanny world, led by my two daughters, their imaginary friends, the strangely familiar ghosts that only they could see and their friendly bedroom neighbourhood, occupied by children intricately made from toilet tubes. Learning rekindles this sense of navigating new understandings and possibilities and so is intimately connected with mothers, especially as part of that negotiation is about what it is to be a woman and to live in the world.

It could be argued that it is the role of education to open us up to the uncanny, the unsettling and the unfamiliar, rather than create cosy homely environments that lull us into a false sense of security. This discussion returns me to the starting point of Chapter 1, the co-existence of the real and the imagined, the necessity of opening up the door to the imagined world, and to the ever changing unself that moves through that door and back again.

> How concrete everything becomes in the world of the spirit when an object, a mere door, can give images of hesitation, temptation, desire, security, welcome and respect. If one were to give an account of all the doors one had closed and opened, of all the doors one would like to re-open, one would have to tell the story of one's entire life. But is he who opens a door and he who closes it the same being?
>
> (Bachelard, op. cit., p. 224)

## Multiple spaces of unacknowledged learning and unrequited love

> It is the elsewhere of discourse here and now, the blind spots, or the space-off of its representations. I think of it as spaces in the margins of hegemonic discourses, social spaces carved in the interstices of institutions and in the chinks and cracks of the power-knowledge apparati.
>
> (de Lauretis 1987, p. 2)

In this next section I want to expand this discussion to explore how education has been spatialized to exclude certain forms of learning as non-belonging.

One of the most important issues that educational researchers need to address, but often ignore, is the learning that is not allowed to count as learning, the forms of knowledge generation that somehow evade the learning communities and communities of practice. This is the learning that takes place in what de Lauretis calls the 'space-off' of the main educational stage. To begin, I want to analyse, as a case, the use of informal spaces of learning amongst some of the young white working class men in my research. This will demonstrate how learning is being respatialized but is also kept hidden and disavowed by policy makers and by dominant discourses. The question is whether these blind spots, cracks and chinks are productive or simply out of the limelight.

## White working class men and informal learning

To return to the discussion in Chapter 1 about the 'self', young white working class men have been constructed mainly as authentic lacking selves, who simply don't have the right inherent 'dispositions' to learn. This rigid structuring of a fixed self ties with an unremitting focus on their prowess in the sites of formal learning. Moving the discussion to more informal learning is synchronous with adopting the 'unself' perspective, where movements into and out of learning might reflect and respond to their fluidity of being.

In media and policy discourse in the UK, young white working class men are dominantly positioned as non-learners exiled from education, with the emphasis placed on low achievement and school exclusion (Cassen and Kingdon 2007; the Social Justice Policy Group 2007). A classic photomontage published by the Times Higher Education Supplement in 2005 summons up the collective consciousness on this issue and presents young confident women in academic gowns juxtaposed with sullen young men withdrawn under their hooded sweatshirts. The accompanying article entitled 'Too cool for school and it's downhill from there', links boys' failure at school with high rates of male dropout from university, and attributes this to the lack of 'learning dispositions' amongst such young men. Exile from education is a downward spiral. The apparent disaffection of young working class men from education, their ensuing lack of employment opportunities, becoming ever more acute under recession, and the social problems that these factors appear to cause are seen as one of the most pressing social and educational issues currently facing the UK and in other contexts such as Canada (Martino 1999) and Australia. However, it is beyond 16 that these issues most embed themselves as social problems, and raise policy dilemmas. Young men are twice as likely to be NEET (Not in Education, Employment or Training), at age 16 than young women are (DCSF 2008). Young white men, especially those from disadvantaged areas outside London, are the least likely young people to go to university and most likely to drop out (National Audit Office (NAO) 2008). Young, white, working class men thus pose the most significant challenge to the aims of the Leitch Review (2006) that *all* young people are to be involved in education and training up to the age of 18.

Policy makers and practitioners are highly aware of this issue and spend much time and energy considering possible solutions (see DCSF 2008). However, the challenge is persistently represented as one of changing minds, cultures and aspirations so that young men can stop being non-learners and start participating in education and training. Rarely is it acknowledged that young men are *already* actively learning and enjoying it, just in different contexts and with different motivations. My analysis seeks to take this marginalized perspective seriously, developing an approach which *recognizes* (rather than misrecognizes) this unrequited love of learning.

Informal learning itself has become in the UK a highly charged policy issue, linked inexorably to a climate of consumerism, and a drive to shift responsibility onto the individual adult for shaping and funding their learning pathway. Thus, while an acknowledgement of informal learning is highly desirable, the motives and consequences of this policy move are rather suspect. The consultation conducted by DIUS on *Informal Adult Learning – Shaping the Way Ahead* was intended to produce a 'new vision for informal adult learning for the 21st century' (DIUS 2008a). The response to the consultation calls for 'targeted research to be commissioned in order to develop a robust evidence base about the benefits of informal learning' (DIUS 2008b, p. 8). However, there have been strong critiques that the consultation itself has tended to ignore many activities that are potentially very important to learners and that the bias is towards the older and more middle class learner (see National Institute for Adult and Community Education (NIACE) 2008). While those in the lifelong learning field have long called for recognition for the significance of informal learning (see, for example, McGivney 1999; Field 2005) there are also deep concerns that an emphasis on unstructured learning activities draws attention from widespread cuts in formal adult learning. Informal learning is thus in danger of becoming a political tool, while the practices of informal learning amongst marginalized groups remain ignored and devalued.

Defining 'informal learning' is certainly problematic. Colley *et al.* (2003) suggest that making a division between formal and informal learning is not helpful. In drawing together the findings of recent Economic and Social Research Council Teaching and Learning Research Programme projects, Fuller and Biesta (2008) argue that whenever formal learning takes place, there is always informal learning happening too. In our research on learning brokerage with the homeless people and young people in community arts organizations, we concluded that people do not necessarily conceptualize their activities as learning at all (Quinn *et al.* 2004), thinking of them more in terms of pleasures and times to enjoy themselves. It can be argued that assigning the tag of 'learning' is the quickest way to stop people wanting to do them, when learning for so many only equates with boredom and irrelevance, as the research with the young people in jobs without training graphically demonstrates:

> My whole thought of GCSEs was a waste of time cause I've not actually had to use them. Ever since I've left school, no one's asked me 'What grades have you got?'
>
> (Liz)

These are important debates but notwithstanding these issues, a useful contextual distinction can be made between learning in formal educational, training or work settings and learning that takes place elsewhere primarily for pleasure. DIUS suggests 'while there is currently no formal definition

of informal adult learning shared across government departments, broadly
we are talking about structured or unstructured part time, non vocational
learning which does not lead to qualifications' (DIUS 2008a). This is the
'informal learning' I am interested in, while recognizing that it is still too
static a conception of what is an amorphous field of activity engaged in by
an ever changing unself. In particular, I am interested in what McGivney
identifies as the third category of informal learning: learning which arises
from the activities and interests of groups, but which may not be recognized
as learning (McGivney 1999). Given the growth of virtual networking since
McGivney's definition, it could now be extended to activities that are conducted with others via electronic media.

There are several significant discourses that position young white working class men as being somehow 'outside' of learning. Masculinity and in
particular 'laddish' masculinities are blamed for encouraging boys' under-
achievement (Jackson 2006), stimulating rebellion and 'hardness' which
encourage peer groups to take pride in resisting schooling (Francis and
Skelton 2005). Being white and working class is also posited as a deficit
position, one of abjection and vulgarity (Haylett 2001) and a legitimate
target for contempt (McDowell 2007). White working class communities
are viewed with fear as sources of decay and backward thinking and within
them young men are positioned as 'feral' youths, both hopeless inadequates
and dangerous purveyors of crime and violence (Quinn *et al.* 2006; Nayak
2006). Educational research suggests that white working class boys' rejec-
tion of education is a reaction to an education system that simply doesn't
love them and is inimical to their needs and that historically has always
linked the working class with failure (Reay 2004; 2006). In contemporary
contexts, middle class families fear that their children's opportunities will
be contaminated by this failure (Reay *et al.* 2007), weighing their own supposed vigilance over educational progression and opportunities against the
families that they believe don't care about education (Hollingworth *et al.*
2007). Pupils who have experienced difficulty in formal education are seen
to exhibit 'spoilt' learner identities (Reay and Ball 1997) and their interests
are seen as illegitimate (Archer *et al.* 2010). My own research showed that
dropout from higher education had become another assumed marker of

working class failure to succeed (Quinn 2004a). While education is associated with 'finding yourself' for the middle classes, it is often experienced as 'losing yourself' for the working classes (Hey 2003; Reay 2001).

Policy makers, predominantly white, middle class, university educated males operating in a metropolitan context, dichotomize masculinity across class lines into highly 'successful' and 'lacking'. Aggression and self-confidence are desirable attributes in parliament, but not on a sink estate. Indeed, politicians address the problem of masculinity with macho threats such as: 'We can crack lad culture' (DfES 2003c). Bhabha argues that this type of polarization is inherent to the construction of masculinity, whose governing terms are contradiction, anxiety and ambivalence: 'Are you a man or a mouse' I can still hear my attorney father repeatedly confronting me in Bombay . . . 'Do I have to choose?' I remember thinking in anxious awkwardness' (Bhabha 2005, p. 58). Our participants were constructed as both too much man and too much mouse; aggressive and hopeless at the same time.

A number of writers have focused on this group of young men and concluded that their reservations about formal learning are quite justified McGivney (2004) and that they are seeking to find alternative spaces, such as the 'sheds' used by older men in Australia, as spaces where they can learn together and escape what they portray as the overly feminized space of education (Golding *et al.* 2004). Although Golding doesn't portray it in those terms, it is imagined social capital, produced by the imagined community of 'real' men,that seems to drive this movement. Other writers have traced the kinds of imagined social capital generated by nostalgia and memory that I discussed in Chapter 3. Michael Young exposed how people deal with 'low status' mundane jobs by developing 'counter values' which validate their own lives and provide a source of hope and aspirations (quoted in Watts and Bridges 2006, who found their participants similarly had community-generated and embedded values and ambitions). This links to the work of Rose (2002) in documenting the intellectual life of the British working classes and the need to develop a contemporary picture of the learning of young white working class men. While not claiming to be able to produce such a picture in this book, I would like to make a contribution towards it, by validating the role of informal learning as an intellectual dimension in such young men's lives.

## Unrequited love

The issue of young white working class men and informal learning has emerged in two of the research studies I am discussing in this book. The existence of male love of learning in informal contexts is also supported by research with a younger cohort in a London setting (Archer *et al.* 2005) and by Watts and Bridges' study (2006) focused in the east of England. I use the word love advisedly, because in talking about these activities the level of commitment and passion was high. Yet it was an unrequited love, since officially learning seems to want little to do with them.

In the study of working class dropout from higher education, the majority of the participants were young white men. These were the success stories who had made it to university, bucking the overall trend for their group. While these were men who had withdrawn from degree courses and from formal education, this did not equate with a negative attitude towards learning. However, the learning which most engaged them had become a forbidden planet. Many had demonstrated a long-term love of learning in alternative spaces such as making music and filmmaking: 'Music was my big thing; I was really into that in a big way.' However, when they had tried to translate this into a career trajectory or channel their formal learning around these interests, this was not well received by others. For example, it appeared that careers advisers and teachers deemed such goals inappropriate for working class men:

I told the Careers people I wanted to make films for a living but they told me I'd never be able to do that. They made me tick boxes on a computer. The number one jobs the computer came up with were stonemason, police officer and mechanic.

(Stewart, Scotland)

Their teachers too employed stereotypes of unruly and dangerous working class masculinity:

> I was an outsider, they encouraged other people but not me . . . It sounds pathetic but my nickname was 'scary Pete', they all thought I was a bit psychotic. I had been in a rough area. I was a bit rough at the time.
>
> (Pete)

They sought to regulate them by mainly channelling these young men into 'suitable' subjects such as computing and engineering, which might lead into career pathways that fitted their gender and class. Ending up on degrees that did not really interest them, they could not sustain their studying and ended up dropping out. The sensible subjects that appeared to fit an orderly progression of the self onto a respectable and appropriate employment became something of a straightjacket and a source of alienation. Whereas they enjoyed flexibility and opportunities to cut across fixed disciplinary categories, this did not seem to be encouraged. In fact an interesting finding of our study was that they were sometimes dropping out of education in order to reconnect with learning and take up these passionate attachments again. Their persistence for learning the things that spurred such passions could be remarkable:

> Stewart: When I left university I worked full-time for eight months. Then I started making films again. I'm working on a Western set in Glasgow.
> Interviewer: Is that something you set up yourself?
> Stewart: My friend and I wrote it. As we wrote it things just got bigger and bigger. We thought we'd see if we could get funding for digital video.
> Interviewer: So what sort of places do you go for funding?
> Stewart: There are a few independent companies in Glasgow. We are going through them.

Similar patterns can be traced amongst white working class men in the study of young people in jobs without training. Although they are considered school leavers who need to be brought back into formal education, the young, white working class men in this study were engaged in multiple forms of informal learning. They were active in activities such as deejaying, making music, computing and in outdoor activities with organizations like the Army Cadets. However, they did not seem to have the confidence or encouragement to develop employment or formal training in these areas, or to believe that these skills marked them out as having abilities. Although we had designed the question 'what are you good at?' to open up discussion of these informal areas and raise confidence, it often seemed to have the opposite effect:

> Interviewer: What are you good at?
> Josh: Don't know really, talking, laughing, don't know, nothing really.
> Interviewer: What are you good at?
> Adam: Don't know, don't know.
> Interviewer: What are you good at?
> Carl: I'm rubbish.
> Interviewer: What are you good at?
> Jamie: Not much.

Since policy only recognizes accredited training as a legitimate target for this group, informal forms of learning become negated and invisible. Moreover, the young people did not connect these sorts of activities with what had been a profoundly unenjoyable school experience. When asked if they could make a connection between their learning at home and the world of college they found it difficult to do. Similarly, there seemed little evidence that the careers advice they were getting took such activities seriously. It seemed much more common for them to be funnelled into customer care or similar non-learning and low level activities.

The creative sector – including films, music, fashion, TV and computer games – is the fastest growing professional area in the UK. Yet the recent all-party report chaired by Alan Milburn MP, *Unleashing Aspirations* (Milburn 2009), demonstrates that for most people chances of getting a job in this sector are more limited than ever. Those with families with high income and good networks now dominate the creative industries, where unpaid internships are becoming the route into employment. My research studies demonstrate how young working class men are being actively excluded from these professions at a very early stage, even when they demonstrate interest and aptitude.

## Responding to personal passions

Moving on to my other studies, for the homeless men, the Basic Skills agenda, which the organization was under pressure to push, and for which the most funding was available, was not what brought them into learning, or generated the possibility of employment. It was rather personal pleasures and enthusiasms that sparked this possibility and their learning support workers were quick to respond:

> When I first came in to this work there was part of me that wanted to give other people the opportunity to do the same thing as me. I had my own personal agenda in that I was going to go out and save souls through this method. That seemed to fit with the institutional agenda of getting people qualifications so they could go and get jobs so they would no longer be a burden on society and the two seemed to marry up quite nicely and I thought the two would work together but they didn't. It's been far more successful when I've been relaxed and let people come, but at the same time let people know what the possibilities are, that they can look at them, much gentler process, a much slower process.
>
> (Sam, learning support worker, homeless organization)

This approach had started to bear fruit, as the learners started to make explicit links between what they enjoyed and potential employment opportunities: 'They're trying to get me a job in a radio station because I use computers for music, that's all I'm interested in' (Phil, homeless learner).

For the arts organizations, informal learning amongst young black men was also a key issue and because they had the support of a strong community-based programme they were being helped to move from 'hobby' to profession in ways that had seemed barred to the men in the other studies.

> Paul: We're working a lot with young men at the moment who have a strong interest in rap but may be developing that interest outside . . . they have their own little networks of young people, young men . . . but they're doing it in very informal and unstructured ways.'
> Leon: To me (the arts project) is more than a hobby but to some people if I explain what I do it sounds like a hobby . . . and that's what I don't like.

(community arts focus group)

My research studies suggest that a framing in terms of love is a fertile and important area for further study and that, when recognized, such passion can generate tangible educational opportunities. In the case of the young white working class men, given that this love of learning was hidden and disregarded, and yet appeared to have potentially strong implications for education and employment, it is ripe for systematic analysis. This shift in emphasis from deficit to plenty and from a punitive to a celebratory approach can help shift current blocks in thinking about education, and potentially place young white working class men at the centre, not at the margins.

## Redefining educational spaces: everyday activities

Such expanding and redefining spaces of learning calls into question the privileging of formal educational institutions and the assumption that only a course with a beginning and end and a certificate to prove it has meaning. Drawing on the work of thinkers such as Freire and Illich, adult educators have a long history of redefining what counts as learning and feminist interventions have helped to take these ideas further. For example, Penny Jane Burke and Sue Jackson have consciously worked to redefine lifelong learning, to take into account what might previously have been devalued and ignored (Burke and Jackson 2007). Postcolonial thinkers have pushed even harder to question which is centre, which periphery and how the everyday lives of marginalized groups often have more to teach than to learn. They highlight the fact that learning is an everyday activity, even in the most inauspicious of settings. For example, research in the shanty towns of Buenos Aires has revealed how these spaces of 'rubbish', 'urban hyper-degraded territories', may be precious spaces of passion, pleasure and learning for those who live in them (Grinberg 2009). A space that is popularly envisioned as somewhere to escape from or transcend may be a space of belonging. In making these statements of belonging, the schoolchildren in the study emphasized pleasure, romance, dance and song as the constituents of their daily lives which held them where they were. Interestingly, fighting too became re-signified as 'romantic' and a significant part of this scenario, suggesting that symbols can be created and manipulated rather than simply being imposed. It is the imagined rather than the real that shapes their experience, although this can only take them so far – they remain physically and socially isolated. Despite the power of the imagined in this case we cannot forget that boundaries exist. We cannot assume that:

> Space is indifferent, that it acts as a fluid medium in which mobile subjects dwell . . . space is not like this. For example there is the matter of boundaries. Boundaries are important. . . . as ways of fixing and displaying the subject by making it impossible to move.
>
> (Pile and Thrift 1995, p. 374)

Although Grinberg's study demonstrated that the children of the shanty town did not want to move, how possible was movement anyway? If the shantytown was demolished would it only be recreated elsewhere? This is one of the dilemmas of the researcher who believes in the power of the symbolic, not to lose sight of the potency of the material and the injustices that form it. It is crucial to acknowledge the interplay of the potential of the imagined with the demands of survival.

Sam: What we've tried to do is always try to work out what they want, what they need, just to get them to engage in some way.

JQ:  So how difficult is it to get that initial engagement?

Sam:  It's very difficult, very difficult.

JQ:  What are the reasons why people won't engage?

Sam:  I think the main reason is because they've really got far more pressing engagements. They've got more important things to do. Being on the street and in hostels it is about survival. It's a tougher world.

(Sam, learning support worker, homeless organization)

In exploring the possibilities of re-imagining educational spaces, I bear in mind de Certeau's idea of diversions and assimilations into systems of domination, as noted in my introductory chapter. Diversions are possible but systems of domination make some assimilation inevitable.

## Re-imagining formal learning spaces

I want now to consider formal educational settings and whether we can re-imagine them in productive ways. Much of the literature on universities emphasizes its role in reproducing inequalities and marginalizing and excluding different groups of people, such as working class or black people. (Archer *et al.* 2003) In researching the daily learning lives of women students, I too found much evidence of such inequality: absence of women in the curriculum, pedagogical approaches which favoured men, cultures of marginalization of working class, black, older and disabled women (Quinn 2003a). However, for the women themselves the space was envisioned quite differently: as discussed previously in this chapter, their language was a language of belonging in which the university, not the home, was the protected space. Trying to understand this contradiction I found Gillian Rose's idea of 'paradoxical space' extremely helpful. The university was configured through their own needs and desires which both resisted and were shaped by the dominant masculine discourse. In this sense it was what Rose terms 'paradoxical space' a 'different kind of space where women need not be victims . . . a space imagined in order to articulate a troubled relation to the hegemonic discourses of masculinism' (Rose 1993,

p. 159). For this space to exist at all it had to be seen as oppositional to the oppressive 'man's world' which they felt they still inhabited elsewhere. Paradoxically, the very conditions of male hegemony and the tools gained in the masculinist space of the university, produce possibilities of resistance. Uses of university space are not linear and rational but both symbolic and material.

The clash between the symbolic negotiations employed by learners and the institutional sense of itself as pursuing logical goals, was highlighted in the research with students who had dropped out. Here we included participative events where lecturers and student support staff were amongst those who discussed their perspectives on retention and reiterated the many initiatives they were involved in, that were designed to help students to stay in the university. There was a palpable sense of frustration that, although a whole raft of initiatives existed to support students and prevent them from withdrawing early, for students themselves, these activities had not attained positive symbolic power. Indeed, there were strong, negative connotations in entering the symbolic order of one who needed support: 'I'm not the kind of person who needs help, I can sort it out by myself.' Signposting and telling students about services did not make them appear meaningful or accessible: 'They said something about it at induction, but I didn't really know where to go.' Dropout itself was a very potent symbol, so powerful that some universities refused to mention it at all, for fear of summoning it up: 'We felt that talking about dropping out at induction would give a negative impression' (careers adviser).

Unlike the women students I studied, who seemed to gain resources from their studies that they could use in building up their imagined social capital, these resources seemed thin on the ground for student dropouts. There may be a variety of reasons for this: for many they had chosen the wrong course and so did not enter disciplines which they felt nourished them. Many of them had been steered onto technical subjects by their schools, such as Computing and Engineering and perhaps these simply offered less opportunity to make symbolic connections with others, unlike the women studying looser interdisciplinary degrees within American Studies or Environmental Studies. All of them were first generation entrants and all of them were young and so different forms of cultural capital and life experience were not available to them.

So if formal educational spaces are not experienced formally by learners how does this compute with the technicist and managerial ethos of contemporary universities? Cameron McCarthy, for example, has argued that there are three dominant neo-liberal tendencies at work in universities: virtualization, vocationalization and fiscalization (McCarthy 2009). If we analyse these tendencies in the light of their potential to generate imagined social capital, the omens are not good. All these tendencies work to homogenize the learning experience. Virtualization tends to flatten the opportunities for engaging with difference and allows the student to avoid aspects of communal life that they may find difficult or challenging. Vocationalization ties the learning experience to a fixed rhetoric of employability, so that there is no time or incentive to get lost and find new geographies of the possible. Fiscalization means that the budget is the bottom line; everything is sacrificed to it and innovations and experimental thinking may be the first casualties.

This does not mean that universities ignore their symbolic resources in pursuing these goals. They are quite adept at playing with them, so websites and prospectuses emphasize virtualization with their many images of students and laptops; they highlight employment categories and future possibilities and they also stress value for money. They also co-opt other consumerist pleasures which are congruent with the principles of virtualization, vocationalization and fiscalization and suggest how being a student improves access to such activities as shopping and clubbing. Indeed, one of the universities I studied in my research on women students very self-consciously marketed itself as the ideal place for 'pleasure loving hedonists'. However, symbolic power is not so easily bought. The women in my study just as resolutely rejected these symbols 'these clubs are just cattle markets' and they chose other pleasures such as snowboarding which gave them a sense of release rather than capture. The university marketed itself as a pleasure dome and tried to anticipate what might keep the students happy and content within it, but some refused to be seduced.

## Open and closed spaces

For those in my studies there were many things they were interested in knowing and learning about, and potentially this knowledge could grow across space and time. However, the knowledge they were provided with in their formal educational settings was often rigidly confined and enforced by complex systems of codes and regulations, designed as much to exclude as to facilitate. Throughout the learner accounts there are images of open and closed spaces of prisons and playrooms.

> . . . there's people at high school who are turning off school, they're being forced to go there, their parents get fined if they don't turn up, that's going the wrong way about it because you're going to create an enemy sort of thing.
>
> (Salah, youth representative arts organization)

I have spoken elsewhere of the 'corporeality of learning' (Quinn 2004c), exploring the role of the body in the education of women students and in the work of educational researchers. There I addressed the significance of the everyday body, not just the body with a disability or body in crisis, as a matter which had been neglected in writing on education. Building on this, I would like to reflect on what my research reveals about embodied desire for knowledge, the moments when energy moves through the body like a flame. There are rare moments where the learners in my studies attained this moment of being in the flow where there are no distinctions between the body knowing/creating and what is being known or created: 'When you are being creative you're learning anyway, you can't help but be learning, you're in that mode, so it's all going on for you' (Leon, arts organization).

Knowing here is like a letting go and an opening up and allowing fluidity to take over. Distinctions between play and learning blur:

> Yes I think of it almost as a playground approach, here's lots of toys, here's lots and lots and lots of toys that we can play with. Let's give them the opportunity to do that and they can find one toy they like more than

another and try to encourage them to look deeper into that and explore that.

(Sam, support worker, homeless organization)

However, much more prevalent are accounts of disassociation – when people feel disengaged and remote from knowledge, as if it had no connection to them. This is produced when strict demarcations are made between what is valid and invalid knowledge. For most of the young people in the jobs without training project, school had been a process of switching off, as a way of managing humiliating and threatening experiences. When they were in primary school they had experienced pleasure in knowledge, but entry into secondary school seemed to cut that off. They felt that that they had became disembodied and undifferentiated in the eyes of teachers and advisers: 'the thick bunch'. Similar processes were at work for the young people who had dropped out of university: 'Here the lecturer doesn't even know if you walk past him. He doesn't even know if you are a student. It makes it hard.'

Once leaving school or university they appear to be engaged in trying to re-assert the body. This can be connective and a way of reclaiming the possibility of knowledge via the employment of physicality: 'I'm not the dumb labourer, I'm a hands-on learner' or it can be a form of disavowal of abstractions and texts in favour of the tangible:

Well at college I prefer it to be more practical and like learning about what you are actually doing but then they are like oh make a poster about health and safety and it's like I don't want to do that.

(Fred)

When I was doing this degree it was like you learn how to make a cup software wise, but there is no purpose to it, there's no reason. Now I learn to make a cup and then I make 50 of them at work and the boss said this is fantastic I didn't know you could do that. And I have improved the time. And you are using it straight away and getting feedback.

(student 'dropout')

The most exuberant account was that of a professional magician where learning, work and sheer love of life seemed to fuse. This pleasure spilled over into the way he responded to his surroundings and wanted to share them with others: 'It's a brilliant place to live, Weymouth, have you ever been here before? Oh absolutely gorgeous we've got all the bays and the scenery' (Rick). This contrasts with the territorial approach of many others where the local space was very undesirable but still had to be kept to themselves: 'It's a bit crap in Launceston. There are about a thousand Polish people taking all the construction jobs and if you haven't got any qualifications you struggle' (Simon).

In some respects, these learner accounts respond to Deleuze and Guattari's (1980) concepts of smooth and striated space, where smooth space allows free movement and fluidity and striated space imposes a grid of boundaries and restrictions. The learners are not naïve about it – they do recognize that different contexts have their own imperatives to closures, and acknowledge that, as Deleuze and Guatari themselves stress, pure smooth space is not possible. Their accounts also evoke Helen Colley's work on time and closures and openings to learning, where the two are held in a permanent contrapuntal relationship:

> We can therefore see the contradictions between closures and openings as an unending and fragmenting process, which is neither linear nor simplistically circular: while one contradiction may be resolved, a new one will surface. We might more accurately depict the process, then, as a number of zigzag or spiral movements within a web of contradictions.
>
> (Colley, op. cit., p. 438)

For those in the voluntary sector organizations, comparing the relative openness of the learning and support they were receiving now, with their experience of more formal establishments, was informed by realism:

> The thing with probation is it has to have rules and guidelines to stick to where here it doesn't, it's open.
>
> (Alan, homeless organization)

Leon:  The tutors here work together with you.

Shania:  Yes but in college teachers have got targets to meet haven't they
and they've got to report to someone so she's got to think of herself
at the end of the day, she's got to report to her principal or head of
department or whatever.

(focus group, arts organization)

The existences of the voluntary sector organizations are predicated on the
limitations of the formal sector; those limitations provide justification for
the voluntary sector work and permit them to exist. However, this knowledge does not prevent a desire for the open space as the one most likely to
facilitate learning and as a necessary possibility:

[the arts organization] is important because *young people feel it's hard in
school* – a place like this gives them a chance to *open up* and do what they
feel they have a skill in whether it be singing, acting, dance, behind the
scenes work . . .

(Leon, my emphasis)

School is hard, closed and restrictive, as opposed to the arts activities which
are open, smooth and generative. In this other space they are allowed to
explore diverse interest and possibilities rather than being perceived as an
undifferentiated mass.

At school education is structured . . . over here it's easier and I don't know
but I would say you learn easier here with all the encouragement that's
around you and the pressures less.

(Gary)

Because I've just finished a BTEC in Performing Arts I wanted to go to
Drama School and stuff and then coming here I realized I don't wanna
go to Drama School because I went to one audition and it was very like
narrow . . . and here it's more open and I do things that I enjoy and not
following a narrow path . . . when I come here I can express myself and

say what I want to say and still feel that I am learning.

(Shania)
(arts organization focus group)

Similarly, in the homeless organization openness helps to break down divisions between teaching and learning, where all are potentially both teacher and learner. This is an issue I shall return to in Chapter 5.

In one arts organization focus group, perennial debates about accreditation emerged. As so many before them have done, students debated whether it is the experience of learning itself, or what it represents retrospectively in the market place, that is the most important:

When I went for an audition at Drama School I ended up thinking that the only good thing about going there would be to *say* that I'd *been* to Drama School, I don't know if the whole three years would have been good, d'you get what I mean?

(Shania)

Those engaged in trying to develop learning opportunities for particularly marginalized people (taking resources out to them and encouraging their participation in public spheres such as libraries) were engaged in lively debates about fluidity and openness, where movement into learning could be lateral and validity was organic and personal:

JQ: Could anyone say what they think learning is?

Sam: In the sense of whether learning something is accredited or recognized as a course then that's not necessarily what learning is about.

Librarian: It's more organic . . . I think people are comfortable now with the ideas of learning being just about acquiring new skills or knowledge regardless of what that is. It's new for that person. They can do something that they couldn't do before or they know something they didn't know before. They've had a learning experience.

Drugs support worker: It's about learning being for the individual as opposed to the individual being forced into a learning structure that doesn't fit . . . I think that's a key, that you say that you can learn in different ways and that it's not necessarily about success or failure, it's about the learning activity in its own right.

Librarian: And the whole idea that people in terms of progression, it can be lateral and that's what suits some people . . . they don't have to go up some sort of ladder. I think people in general tend to be lateralists, they tend to like to move that way.

(Focus group discussion, steering group library outreach project)

Nevertheless, this grassroots knowledge does not appear to be very influential when it comes to designing and administering formal education and qualifications. Structures remain hierarchical and stratified and qualifications are the measure of success. In this climate there can be no real resolution of the accreditation debate, and the reality for learners is that to survive and progress they must negotiate a very fragile line between doing what they want and what powerful others deem they should. What can be said is that the possibilities offered by the 'border zone' must be protected so that learners can decide for themselves how and when to move from learning for pleasure to accreditation and back again:

So we're not trying to water down their creative interest, but we're trying to say there's a place that's interested in what you're doing, that can offer professional support and can encourage you to think about further and higher education. So the 'border zone' is really that type of approach.

(Paul, tutor, community arts organization)

It is not helpful to refute all forms of accreditation; that is a luxury only the highly qualified can afford. Nevertheless, the fear is, that moving what is healthy and open in voluntary sector practice into a more formalized space, runs the risk of destroying it:

We've been through a phase where mentoring and informal support received some acknowledgement and support . . . so if it has value then it needs some funding support and if we give you some funding support we need you to track and monitor and show results . . . and it's a bit like clockwork orange. The reason it's called clockwork orange is you take something that's organic, juicy, full of life and works and people enjoy and you turn it into this horrible clockwork monstrosity that's got cogs and wheels and has to churn out results that satisfy funders.

(focus group discussion outreach steering group)

## Finding a space to land

In negotiations of space and belonging, movement and stasis form a complex pattern. For the young people in jobs without training there were many images of them circling around space, looking like they might find a place to be comfortable and settle and then starting off again. Neighbourhoods became contested and often dangerous spaces where claims to belong were insecure. They would avoid certain areas or people: 'There's B that's down the valley, but I don't go down there' (Tamara). Territorial battles were fought over ever more scrappy pieces of land. Whatever the manoeuvres their opportunities to leave the locality were limited and tended to be short-lived: 'I went up to Birmingham for a week, but then I came back' (John). Unsuccessful educational histories are not the only, or even the main, reason for these patterns of insecurity, but they do contribute to them.

This contrasts with Popkewitz's (2007) vision of the 'unfinished cosmopolitan' who feels that their education both entitles and facilitates their expansion across the globe in search of even more learning opportunities. However, given the global recession and the need to curtail travel because of climate change this mobile citizen is becoming anachronistic. It is possible that the use of new technologies may bring these two groups, the unfinished cosmopolitan and what we might call the thwarted parochialist together into a new configuration. As Cameron McCarthy (2009) has argued it is the hallmark of the new citizen to be 'vicariously active', self-contained within the enclosed space of the home and organizing their life through mobile technologies. This new citizen is able to move in the world while being completely still. However, capacities to plunder the world do of course remain unequal, as McCarthy makes clear. Without substantially more resources, most of the people I have researched will never attain a form of cosmopolitan mobility in which they feel entitled to access all areas.

## Reclaiming the waste of space

Finally, I want to consider the symbolic casting of some people (and some knowledges) as a 'waste of space', 'waste products' and 'trash', what de Certeau calls 'the "waste products" of a functionalist administration (abnormality, deviance, illness, death, etc.)' (de Certeau, op. cit., p. 95). In doing so I want to explore the ways in which this detritus can be reclaimed and recouped as beautiful, as the 'tough spikey ugly flower' found on the roadside by a factory is, in Allen Ginsberg's poem 'In back of the real' (2006).

Wray and Nevitz's concept of 'white trash' is quite useful here for understanding how the young people in jobs without training were positioned and also many of the young people who had dropped out of university and the homeless people. 'The white trash stereotype serves as a useful way for blaming the poor for being poor' (Wray and Nevitz 1997, p. 1), in that the negative things that happen to them are seen as the inevitable consequence of their own backwardness and vulgarity.

The symbolism of waste runs throughout the learners' accounts, most vividly in those of the homeless people: 'I'm from Yorkshire and it was a shit life for me up there, I'd been in and out of jail and I was a heroin addict when I came and I wanted to get away from my life there' (Cal, homeless project). Yorkshire is both a symbol of all that is shit and a place where shit happens; it has to be left before a process of renewal and change can begin. However these are not linear but cyclical accounts – we and he know that Yorkshire is always there as a likely place of return – even though there seems no reason for Cal to go back. So there is a strong sense of those who are homeless being drawn into negative space, into the black holes of their past and into waste in all its senses: 'If I'm bored and fed up and I've got time to kill I just get wasted' (Alan). Nevertheless, despite the power of this pull, the homeless learners, supported by their project workers, resist and repudiate this symbolic positioning:

> I think the idea of 'the cycle of homelessness' has become an accepted totem and I'm not sure anyone has examined it that closely. They seem to me to be so filled with assumptions . . . it seems to me to have a fundamental disrespect for people's lifestyles . . . What I'm about is if you want to change your lifestyle here's an opportunity, here's an avenue to change it. If you're happy doing that then I'm not going to be judgemental, I'm not going to say you're a failure.
>
> (Sam, learning support, homeless organization)

> I've met guys on the street that have got university degrees and letters after their name and they are classed as down and out and yet they are probably more intelligent than a lot of those people who stick their nose up as they walk past you.
>
> (Alan, homeless charity, focus group)

If we look at the policy rhetoric on young people in jobs without training the recurrent lament is also about wasted lives. Young people who are not engaged in education or training are 'wasting their potential' (DCFS 2008). The Connexions advisers we worked with on the research project often bought into this mindset too, as did many of the stakeholders from local authorities, education training and youth work that we involved in a participative seminar.

The lesson here is that what is garbage to some is useful material to others. For the Connexions advisers, the young people were seen as wasting away and 'drifting and desperate'. For the young people, the same experiences of moving away from formal education can be experienced as a pleasurable period of liminality: 'I want to pass on thoughts of college. I just want to float' (Abi). For many of the Connexions advisers, the young people were prevented from moving forward and perfecting the self-made self by the inherent limitations of the authentic self and its stupidity and laziness, and by the inescapable self which had been shaped by families considered to be without aspirations. The young people themselves had a different perspective. The jobs that others saw as wasting their time and energies were often perceived as enjoyable, productive and interesting – something to be proud of, not ashamed about:

> speaker 1:  What do you do in a typical day?
> speaker 2:  Strimming, hedging and planting people's gardens, not big work . . . It's good, I enjoy it. It makes me feel proud when I stand back and look at the finished job.
>
> (Gary)

While they were cast as non-learning experiences because they did not involve accredited training, the young people themselves often felt they were learning a great deal and building their skills and capacities in very relevant ways. While some of the young people saw their jobs as boring, frustrating and pointless, this is definitely not the whole story. Of course, these observations need not be taken strictly at face value, they may be justifications and obfuscations, but they certainly formed a consistent thread in the ways that the young people presented their relation to work. They exhibited firm resistance to their usual sidelining as nothing more than a waste of space.

For those students who had left university early the discourse of waste was also pervasive. Student 'dropouts' had become respectable by attaining university, but only partially as these universities were often devalued as 'ex-polys'. They had then taken on white trash connotations by dropping out and becoming waste. It is worth noting that Frank Furedi's (2009) book is entitled *Wasted* and fulminates against what he perceives as the dumbing down of university education to the level of trash. The ex-students knew that they were seen as having wasted time, wasted their own future. 'When you say you have dropped out of uni they think you're just a waster' (student from Scotland). The research jury days confirmed that student dropouts are commonly considered irresponsible and unfit to carry out the tasks of citizenship: 'I sit on recruitment panels for local charities and up until today I would have disregarded people who had dropped out for appointments to the voluntary sector' (participant, research jury day).

Non-completion is a waste of talent and resources and we expect HEIs to see what action they can take to help students. The government expects all institutions to bear-down on non-completion and in particular to work with those institutions with higher completion rates.

(DfES representative, quoted in Tarleton 2003)

Anticipating this public response, the students who had left early often kept their university experience from others, such as potential employers: 'I will probably hide it away'. They themselves believed university had not been a waste. It had been a time of reassessment, of thinking through what they did and didn't want to do and what was possible, given constraints such as family financial problems. It had not destroyed desire for education and all but one wanted to return to university in the future. Rather than being detritus and rubbish, the experience had facilitated skills and confidence as the following three ex students attest:

I didn't feel like a failure . . . the job I'm doing now is directly related to the course I was doing. I feel that I achieved something from it.

I think it still set me up and prepared me for life. I didn't feel any shame.

Before I was one of those people who didn't use to talk to many people. Now I'm really open and I have a lot of avenues. I'm quite happy now about going to university.

I know I can make my own decisions. I was always a bit dubious about that. Now I know I can do things for myself.

I wouldn't look at it as positive or negative. I just look at it as a learning curve.

(student 'dropouts')

In such statements the students deflect anticipated criticisms of their early withdrawal. They are both aware of the discursive framework of failure and shame and willing to replace this closed narrative with one of openness, learning and progress. Most were willing to be self-critical and take responsibility for their own mistakes. Instead of employing a narrative of blame of the failed university, one which is very much available to them in popular discourse, they put the period at university into the broader context of their life ahead.

The discourse of waste had also surfaced in my original study of women students. Here it was feminism itself and by extension my research project that was positioned as compost and manure:

> When I said I wanted to do ecofeminism for my final year project he practically laughed me out of the room he said 'what!' and he wouldn't look me in the eyes . . . and he was practically, maybe he didn't mean it, but he was like disregarding anything you'd come up with (in my research project) before he'd ever read anything you'd done and the other tutor was saying 'you've got to sort out the institution, you've got to be really careful where you work, otherwise the institution's going to laugh at you and say what a pile of old manure or compost or something', and I was like 'For God's sake no!'
>
> (Lisa, focus group, Environmental Studies, Expanding University)

Although this disavowal by powerful men was difficult to negotiate for both Lisa and myself, she did do what she wanted for her dissertation and I did do what I wanted for my PhD. The obvious riposte to their comments is that compost and manure help new seeds to grow. Moreover, eight years on from this study, in a world on the verge of environmental collapse, ecofeminism possibly does not seem such a crazy idea.

In all these acts of resistance I find a demonstration that even waste can be reconstituted as valuable. However, it cannot be easily commodified and sold to others. Homeless people do not have much credit in our society and neither do young people who work in shops, students who drop out of university or even ecofeminists. The challenge is to work so that others can see the value of those they overlook, the dusty, dirty flowers of the world, and reshape their practices to work with and not against this value. In the following chapter I will explore how this revisioning can be done.

## Conclusion

The purpose of this chapter has been to create a discussion of home and belonging in relation to educational spaces and also to explore the potential for respatializing learning as fluid so that all learners can find a place to belong. In it I have addressed the multiple meanings and locations of 'home' and considered how learning either generates or threatens protected spaces for learners. I have drawn on spatial theories to understand how the learners in my study are moving through and imagining home and learning. Which space is 'the protected space' is influenced by age, gender and race, with universities offering a space for dreaming for women students, but a mutilation for young black men. The pretensions that formal institutions make to family values are compared with the reciprocal familial relationships that are possible in more informal settings. The chapter also discusses how learners negotiate their relationships to their home towns and the impacts of localities and homelessness on learning experiences. My discussion of belonging embraces the question of the uncanny and not being at home in the world and shows how the uncanny figures in the relationships between women and their mothers, which are intrinsically bound to their ideas and experiences of learning. In the second part of this chapter I move to explore how multiple spaces of learning are experienced. I begin by focusing on informal learning using as a focus the positioning of young white working class men and the ways in which their love of learning is ignored and disavowed. I then investigate the relationships between smooth and striated space across the different spaces of learning and implications for the accreditation of learning. The chapter concludes by tracing how the leitmotif of 'waste' runs through these research studies and addresses how all the learners in their different ways are being placed into this category. Finally it demonstrates that while the learners in my study are overwhelmingly positioned as a 'waste of space' who are not able to belong in reputable learning communities, they themselves are actively resisting this positioning and staking their claim to belong. My aim in the next chapter is to show how waste can be recouped and reformulated into value, by means of ecological thinking.

Chapter 5

# The Joy of Knowledge

## What does knowledge taste like?

In this chapter I want to move forward from the images of waste and detritus I have been exploring towards a cultural and ecological theory of learning, which will recoup and make waste into value, drawing on the work of feminist philosopher Lorraine Code and her 'ideas that dream' (Bachelard 1994, p. 112). Here I want to explicitly concentrate on knowledge. Talking about knowledge is extremely difficult, and indeed is something that many shy away from as too abstract and complex. The image of knowledge as being like the sea: 'Dark, salt, clear, moving, utterly free', which is employed by Elizabeth Bishop (1991) in her poem 'At the Fishhouses', is helpful in visualizing, even tasting, knowledge. I will keep this image in mind as I am writing this chapter. The sea image also takes me back to my discussions about the self. The sea is not only a good image for knowledge but also a metaphor for the unself. Who can say where the sea starts or begins, how deep it is, what colour it is where it is flowing, all these factors are constantly changing. We can name the sea 'the sea', but we cannot contain its mystery. Perhaps this is why so many of us feel drawn to sit and look at the sea for hours, as I have done this summer in Cornwall and Donegal, taking consolation from its unfathomable nature. Rather than being drawn to the sea because it is mighty and different, perhaps we are attracted to its mirroring of our own flux of being.

What is learning about if it's not about knowledge – but knowledge washes away from sight and like the unself is hard to talk about. While social shifts in learning, such as widening participation in higher education, are recognized and adumbrated, implications for the curriculum and for the sorts of knowledge new students might hope to find are little explored. Debates about pedagogy, teaching and learning strategies and student support abound, but thoughts about the subject are missing. Lack of attention in the literature mirrors huge gaps in policy documents. Very little attention is paid to what students learn once they enter university. For example, in widening participation policy documents the word most conspicuous by its absence is 'curriculum': emphasis instead is on 'aspiration', 'access' and 'attainment' (Quinn 2006).

The relationship between social changes, learning transformations and the academic subject has been a central concern of mine since *Changing the Subject* (Davies *et al.* 1994) and continued in more depth in *Powerful Subjects* (Quinn 2003a) and my work on subjects and subjectivities (Quinn 2005b). Here, I want to extend the debate to the particular issues raised by lifelong learning across a range of educational domains. Lifelong learning poses a particular epistemological challenge. While there is no consensus about what it is and how to define it, an idealized vision does exist of learning permeating all spaces and spheres, spanning and responding to all ages and stages of a person's life. For some, this is a neo-liberal nightmare, in which learning is an enforced project of never being 'educated' enough. For others, there is real possibility of breaking down established boundaries between formal and informal learning worlds. Whatever the emphasis of the vision, be it utopian or dystopian, it poses a concomitant challenge to knowledge. If learning is so different and fulfils a different function for the learner, then what they should know must be different. If learning is radically different then what *can* be known must be different too.

Feminist and postcolonial theorizations have exposed how far dominant constructions of knowledge, as enshrined for example in the university curriculum, are bounded and limited by race, gender and class. Each subject:

> Partook of the viewpoint of what was then said to be – and by many is still said to be – the sum total of our cultural heritage; or alternatively, that portion of our cultural heritage that should be preserved. The prose and

poetry, the narratives and theories, the conceptual structures and methodologies of Western Culture that the curriculum was expected to hand down to future generations was authored by the educated white man, for the educated white man, and about the educated white man and his world, or, if about other people and their worlds, from his perspective.

(Martin 1994, p. 224)

Theoretically, lifelong learning, which seeks to escape the formal boundaries of institutions and qualifications, may provide a more open space for new and different forms of knowledge to be recognized and may challenge this dominant worldview and its insidious shaping of academic life. However, since notions of what is permitted and counted as knowledge are culturally embedded and circulated, this sense of opening may be an illusion.

There is no such thing as neutral knowledge that can be held separate from the culture it serves. How possible is it then to change dominant cultural constructions of valid knowledge? Strong challenges have indeed been posed to the 'masters' knowledge. Feminism is predicated on challenging received masculinist ideas about what counts as significant knowledge and where it might be found. Indeed, positioning women as being able to know worthwhile, and possibly different, things is a gauntlet laid down by feminism. Concepts such as the 'malestream curriculum' (Bowles and Duelli-Klein, 1983) have unpicked the supposedly neutral contents of university disciplines, demonstrating how the mainstream is actually a narrow tributary. Black feminism adds a powerful political dimension, with knowledge a tool in shifting power relations (see, for example, Hooks 1994; Lorde 1984). Here the function of dominant forms of knowledge is to construct groups of people as 'other' and legitimate their subservience, and Western feminism itself is not exempt from these practices. Such knowledge cannot be used against itself: 'the master's tools cannot dismantle the master's house' (Lorde 1984). The emergence of queer theory calls into question and destabilizes everything we think we know, including the foundational existence of male and female. It queers our understanding, bringing transgressive understandings forward from the margins, as new and illuminating forms of knowledge (see, for example, Probyn, 1996). Postcolonial theory forces us to recognize the global and historical forces of knowledge structures, in which some cultures are placed at the centre and some on the periphery (see, for example, Alexander, 2005). It recognizes a potential shift in knowledge dominance from West to East and explores the multiplicity of forms knowledge might take: where myth, story and song become as legitimate as the written word (see, for example, Grinberg 2009).

Yet, how far has all this thinking really impacted on what counts for knowledge within mainstream education in the UK? Have assumptions about what is real, worthy of study, central to knowledge, fundamentally changed? I fear not. As a conference participant recently concurred, when I discussed this issue: 'Yes, the show is still on the road'. What Minh-ha calls the 'territorialized knowledge' of the white, the male and the middle class, still steers the show and: 'secures for the speaker a position of mastery, I am in the midst of a knowing, acquiring, deploying world – I appropriate, own and demarcate my sovereign territory as I advance' (Minh-ha 1990, p. 327).

My study with women students was centrally concerned with this issue of knowledge transformation, by exploring the impact of feminist ideas on the mainstream curriculum in higher education. It revealed that although feminism has been an extremely significant intellectual movement, this had not been sufficient to overturn the dominant paradigms of what counts as knowledge in the interdisciplinary subjects I studied. Feminist ideas are incorporated or enclosed within small discrete spaces:

> Within my American Studies module Metropolis there is not much mention of women. I think this was the only week that they have specifically addressed the very masculinised way that predominates when looking at the city. Although this week we were told about books written by women which are trying to redress this view we were not told anything other than the name and title. However, as I am taking two modules on feminism it is quite nice that women's issues are not focused on.
>
> (Jenny, American Studies, Expanding University, diary)

or they are simply ignored and sidestepped:

Tracey: In History and Politics there weren't any women so of course they aren't mentioned.

J. Q.: Well they may not have been in power but they were there.

Joanne: There were women involved but they didn't have the confidence to write, so of course they wouldn't appear. There are no women in History because men wrote all the books.

(Pleasant College, American Studies focus group discussion)

or actively excluded:

Katy: A lot of modules are about the Third World, but when you're talking about the US or Europe you're talking about men.

J. Q.: So you're saying there's not much about women scientists and the work that they have done?

Katy: No and just to be downright awkward I did my poster project on women scientists.

J. Q.: How did that go down?

Katy: They all went 'Who?!' (laughs)

J. Q.: And who was it?

Katy: Barbara McClintock.

(Katy, Environmental Studies, Pleasant College, interview)

The perpetuation of 'common sense' notions about truth and validity, and the continued domination of imperial modes of thought and behaviour that I witness every day in the university sector all cause me to doubt that other seminal theories have had any more impact than feminism has done. This leads me not to reject the theories and the need for theorization, but to recognize the stupefying power of intellectual vapidity and laziness and the reproductive power of vested interests and structures of inequality.

## Materializing love of knowledge

Perhaps a better move is not to theorize *about* knowledge but theorize *from* knowledge. By this, I mean that taking a different vantage point, working outwards from how love of knowledge emerges, rather than theorizing about what knowledge *should* be, may produce more change in how education is understood and delivered. My research studies reveal a love of knowledge warring with a hatred of Education. The challenge, it seems, is how to harness the potential of this seemingly doomed love affair. To do so means materializing, rather than abstracting: to go back to the poem I quoted earlier, what does this love of knowledge 'taste' like?

Elizabeth St Pierre has done some important work in this regard, drawing on Deleuze and Guatari's ideas of smooth and striated space which were discussed in the previous chapter. She has developed the idea of 'smooth mental space' and tries to describe what it feels like to be in it. This is a space that is often entered while doing something else; it catches us unawares, surprising us as we go about some other business: 'It's an affirmative joyous space, perhaps the most thrilling of all the fields in which we work . . . I often found myself moving into it as I took my early morning walks down littered sidewalks' (St Pierre 1997, pp. 371–2).

When we are in this zone our thoughts expand, we are able to think creatively and our bodies fill with delight as we appear to enter a different dimension. Although St Pierre is specifically talking about academic work, I can find many instances of 'smooth mental space' amongst my research participants and it is not confined to those studying at a higher level or to those who have relatively stress-free lives: 'The times I'm here take on a different meaning and I feel totally absorbed . . . you're driving home thinking about things. It puts another dimension in my life' (Joanne, American Studies student); 'I come here and produce music on the computers. It relaxes me and takes everything out of my head' (Pete, homeless charity learning centre).

There is something deeply satisfying and seductive about these images of smooth mental space. Yet, there is also something individualistic and solitary about them too which has recently started to bother me. Is this solipsistic

Shangri-la enough? Where is the mutuality and the communal generation of knowledge? If the master's knowledge is individualistic and territorial what can we know as a free group of women and men?

## Ecological thinking

A further approach is to adopt what Lorraine Code calls ecological thinking (Code 2006). Ecological thinking works on the premise that as we have had to find a different, more holistic, way to understand the interconnectedness of all things in the world, then we must extend this approach to our very ways of thinking about these things, our methodological approaches to researching these things and our conceptualizations of what counts for knowledge. This appears to offer another more relational way in which we might materialize joy of knowledge and build on this to make change. Having found Code's earlier work *What can she know?* (Code 1991) very important in developing my ideas on positionality and the situated construction of knowledge, this new turn in her thinking was a way of drawing many elements together. For me it also coincides with a new personal interest in, if not necessarily conversion to, agnostic Quaker practice, with its concern to 'live adventurously' as a 'seeker' and to attend to the small challenges of everyday life, as well as to global injustice and to constantly make the links between the two.

Ecological thinking provides an alternative theory of knowledge, which, in my view, draws together and synthesizes pre-existing ideas in feminist theorizing in a helpfully thoroughgoing way. As Code formulates it, ecological thinking is not simply a matter of talking about the environment or ecology, it is thinking afresh how we engage with knowledge and doing so in a way that changes theory and practice. This approach has a number of key factors: it is inter/transdisciplinary; it sees all things as interdependent; it argues that small things matter and that diversity must be preserved and respected; it takes a cooperative, participatory approach to knowledge, rather than seeing it as the product of an autonomous isolated reasoner; knowledge is seen as relational, not individualistic, the effects of power in shaping forms of knowledge have to be accounted for, at both local and global levels; knowledge must be generated creatively not destructively, connecting knowing and action; it contests and infiltrates what Code calls the entrenched 'social imaginary' and its governing beliefs about the nature of knowledge and who is allowed to know:

> Ecological thinking reconfigures relationships all the way down . . . it is differently sensitive to the detail and larger patterns of human and 'natural' diversity than the epistemologies of mastery have been: it evoked criteria and standards of knowing well that do in fact seek and respect empirical evidence, while urging another, arguably better way of imaging knowledge and its place in socio-political geographic structures.
>
> (Code 2006, p. 47)

Code's conjoining of respect for empirical evidence, with the drive to imagine knowledge differently, accords very well with my own project in this book. I want to use her ideas to address the research participants in my studies and to see if they can help create a new knowledge paradigm for them.

I want to start with the young people in jobs without training. Through the lens of mastery these young people are nothing but the 'thick bunch'. They know nothing worth knowing, they have no qualifications, no training and no future. The social imaginary positions valid knowledge as formal and accredited, and the young people as 'unknowledgeable' people who must be fixed. It ignores structural inequalities that limit access to accredited knowledge and ignores their love of learning in informal spaces and the relational aspects of that love. This lens of mastery condemns these young people to a deficit position and offers them no way forward, unless they meekly bow to the master's hand. However, taking the position of ecological thinking, what positive relationships can be generated by abandoning the master's position and instead attending to the relational dimensions of the young people's own positionings? What do they want to know together and what are the connections generated by this?

Rather than seeking accredited and tabulated knowledge, they want knowledge that frees them up from the striated space of the classroom and that they can put to use in everyday work: 'I like to learn at work without teachers' (Andrew). They want knowledge they can use for the self and with others. Knowledge becomes interactional and an aspect of their social being, a site of enjoyment:

> I like to do something different, I'm more of a people person really. I like to get there and chat to people, there's so many interesting people out there you know . . . I'm really lucky because I've got a residency in a nightclub in Weymouth and I'm working for them every Saturday evening and that's brilliant as well.
>
> (Rick)

Knowledge is not a mode of differentiation, positioning them as superior to vulnerable others, but a tool whereby they can love to help those others:

> I never planned to stay in the last job (shop) very long. I have always wanted to work with people in this sort of thing but cause I didn't do that well at school I ended up doing that other job in the shop to tide me over. This (working with people with learning disabilities) is what I really want to do . . . I really, really love the work, everything about it is really rewarding I just love it.
>
> (Rose)

They want knowledge that responds to the suffering of self and others:

> A lot of people struggle . . . A few people I've met say they've broken up with their families, they've hated their life and they've tried to do stupid things . . . I don't know why they do it but they've cut themselves . . . One of the people I know I got them to promise not to cut themselves or drink.
>
> (George)

Here we have a knowledge paradigm which is applied rather than formalized, takes account of pleasure and takes account of social relations. It is a knowledge which allows for love and joy. This is not the knowledge being offered up to these young people. As discussed in Chapter 2, the current emphasis is on the accredited skills agenda, an agenda that puts the need for qualifications and training ahead of the need to know something that is individually meaningful. This is limited in itself, and what it appears to deliver in practice is low level and anachronistic programmes which do not engage and take them precisely nowhere and also make the assumption that they have no skills to begin with.

Homeless learners are positioned even more negatively. They are specks of dust in the master's lens, abject and threatening. The social imaginary positions them as beyond knowledge altogether, or as having dark and anti-social forms of knowledge. They must submit to abuse in order to negotiate daily life: 'I think having to deal with different views of the public makes you strong. You have to be polite no matter what they say and not be sharpish back' (Sally). Spatially, they are positioned so far away from centres of elite knowledge that they might as well not exist:

> Universities have never contacted me about whether I have any potential students for their courses or talked to me about what they look for in students or given me promotional materials. I think it's because of a perception that some of the people I'm working with are a million miles away from university but they're not. They may be a year away from university. Many of them could take an access course and could be at Oxford University this time next year, that's how far away they are.
>
> (Sam, learning support worker, homeless organization)

From an ecological perspective, how can this negativity and these destructive assumptions be challenged in order to create conditions of harmony in which they are allowed respect and a rightful place? What do these learners want to know with others? Their desire for knowledge is again led by pleasure. According to their learning support workers, the most popular classes that had been run for them had been university level lectures on body art – a subject in which they had a genuine interest and with which they had no problems engaging on a sophisticated intellectual level. They wanted to expand their horizons and make new connections and develop existing ones:

Can I just make a point though that one of the first reasons why they [the homeless organization] introduced computers here, like if you're living on the streets or you're living in hostels you get to meet a lot of people but a lot of the time you break contact with those people because people move around so it was an option where you could open up email addresses and keep in touch with people.

(Alan)

Creativity is important and is part of their everyday way of being in the world, rather than being a specialist enclave:

I have done a lot of work with this client group in the past and they're a really wonderful bunch of people who have some fantastic skills and abilities and I want to be able to provide a quality service to them . . . They do have a lot of amazing skills and strengths. They have amazing social skills. Incredibly creative I find. People feel a lot more confident with music and art.

(Tania, outreach support worker)

They wanted to share knowledge amongst themselves and facilitate it with others:

Sally: Well in here I think you feel more comfortable, you've got your friends around, if you're stuck with something Cal will help me it's just relaxed.

J. Q.: How did you feel about learning from Cal?

Sally: I had no problem with it at all . . . if it was a teacher or a person in the library I might feel a bit more embarrassed to ask them really.

Cal: Because we know what we are doing one of us can show other people well this is how you do it.

J. Q.: So you're all like teachers and learners as well?

Cal: We can teach what we learn. At the end of the day it's about helping the homeless to help themselves and then we can help ourselves when we're on a better level than say some of the more vulnerable people then we can help them, it's just all about helping each other.

(focus group, homeless organization)

They wanted to be able to make positive interventions in the lives of those who could experience similar problems:

> My volunteering is befriending, going round schools telling them about homelessness and drug addiction and about my life and how I've turned myself around. I'm thinking about going to AA meetings because that's about being able to present yourself and talk . . . presenting yourself and talking to people around you about your situation.
>
> (Cal)

> I want to do some kind of helping other people with drug problems and things like that.
>
> (Sally)

Their potential knowledge project therefore was both intense and wide ranging and it contained both creative elements that might add new dimensions to their lives and elements firmly grounded in their everyday funds of experience. They themselves were a valuable knowledge resource for others. Although their learning support workers tried hard to respond to these needs and desires, funding followed the limited view that basic skills was the only agenda for such people:

> There's a massive assumption about academic ability and their levels of literacy. It's more diverse than anywhere else that I've been to. There's some highly intelligent highly literate people and there are some people that have very low levels of literacy.
>
> (Sam)

While ecological thinking is alert to nuance and difference, learning support systems cannot seem to adapt themselves to complexity.

Taking these examples of the young people in jobs without training and the homeless learners, one thing that stands out is a desire to know on behalf of others. Whereas the thrust of the educational system is towards competition and consumption, a need to know better or more, here we have a need to know for. It seems that knowledge can include knowledge of the vulnerability of others and can kindle a desire to help. This was also echoed in the research with young people in community arts organizations:

> Before I came here it was just I wanted to be an actor and a singer, but coming here and seeing other aspects, like I did Pupil Referral Unit and I've developed more understanding of why they're in PRU . . . like for instance some people not just because they're disruptive in school but some people because they're late . . . so you have more understanding for those people in those situations and I'm more patient . . . we're like mentors . . . I want to be more involved with Youth Arts and stuff like that, help young people to get to places like this.
>
> (Leroy, community arts organization)

Knowledge can also be indebted to others. The women students in my higher education study, particularly those who were mature and working class, recognized that their achievements were dependent on others, such as their networks of family and friends: 'I think if I get this degree there should be ten names on it because I just couldn't do it without them. Our Sharon, my sister, says how's our degree coming on?'

> (Katy)

Without relations of mutuality with others, knowledge became blocked by hierarchies, whereas joint participation generated co-production of valuable knowledge:

> I did the same course and I had to leave . . . partly because the teacher didn't treat us on a level, she was one of those 'I am this person and you are that person' and that was hard 'cause from school you get that but you're more tolerant . . . but when you get to college there should be more

respect between you. And there was none of that really.

(Leon)

Yes our Btec tutors were very elusive sort of turned up occasionally and had this mystical air about them . . . I think you can have as many qualifications as you can count on two hands but I don't know if that always makes a difference . . . I now have a deep sort of want for writing music for films and theatres and I've really crystallized that through being here.

(Don)

(focus group discussion, arts organization)

If ecological thinking is applied to my research data, it seems that there is potential for creating ecological modes of learning in which all learners have a place and can belong to a harmonious whole. Although it may be dismissed as wishful thinking, there is evidence here that the kinds of knowledge people want and the ways that they want to gain it can be marked by generosity and cooperation and a desire to leave the world a better place than when they found it. The problem is that we do not live in an ecologically sound environment, but one which is poisonous and destructive. As Žižek argues, we are all now what Ranciere calls the 'part of no-part' of the social body:

> What unites us is that, in contrast to the classic image of proletarians who have 'nothing to lose but their chains', we are in danger of losing ALL: the threat is that we will be dispossessed of our symbolic substance, with our genetic base manipulated and vegetating in an unliveable environment . . . The figure of the 'part of no part' confronts us with the truth of our position, and the ethico-political challenge is to recognise ourselves in this figure. We are all excluded from nature as well as from our symbolic substance.
>
> (Žižek 2009, p. 32)

As I discussed at the beginning of this chapter, knowledge is shaped by dominant frames and learning cannot be a separate space apart from culture. The ecological paradigm has only had lip service paid to it as yet.

## Back to the sea: Cosmic belonging

*I am remembering a vulnerable young woman with learning difficulties, wearing a pink sweatshirt, walking alone in Derry, in the empty streets by TkMax. A young woman that my friend Ann knows. I would like to create a world of safety and belonging for her – an ideal world of harmony. I know it doesn't exist and I know that she is not a passive creature to be done to. Working with her, rather than for her, and seeking a better world for both of us, in recognition that this is a never ending process, not a completion, is a better vision and one to aspire to.*

*(J. Q., research diary)*

At the end of this chapter I want to return to the image of the sea that I introduced earlier and to do so via another poem, 'On the beach at night alone' by Walt Whitman (1964). In this poem there is an idealized glimpse of ecological relationships in which worlds, beings, differences and connections are held together across time, space and distance and where 'A vast similitude interlocks all'. This beach is very different from the classroom. It is a privileged vantage point from which to grasp the 'vast similitude', which the everyday workings of systems and procedures block from our view. Necessarily, perhaps, as otherwise all would grind to a halt to make way for the charm of reflection. Nevertheless, this reflection is not a luxury but a necessity, as Code's (2006) thinking demonstrates. Having covered different forms of belonging, we are left with cosmic belonging. This belonging is very different in nature than belonging in a learning community, where all are expected to be the same. It values and supports difference as necessary for the perpetuation of the globe, never mind the classroom. Perched on the planet, we have no option but to take its survival seriously. Ecological thinking and learning, where the value and beauty of all living things is recognized and facilitated, including such flotsam and jetsam as the marginalized people in my studies, is truly the only way left for us to go.

# Conclusion

In this chapter I have sought to escape the discourse of waste that has haunted the lives and learning of my research participants. My approach has been to excavate the materiality of the joy of knowledge, using Code's (2006) ideas of ecological thinking. I begin by recognizing the difficulty in grasping and embodying knowledge, using a sea metaphor to convey its fluid nature. The potential for lifelong learning to challenge the 'masters' knowledge is discussed, but the limited impact of feminism, black feminism, queer theory and postcolonial theory on mainstream education is recognized. Instead of a focus on how knowledge should be constructed I adopt a different approach, considering how a joy of knowledge is materialized by learners and what potential for change this poses. However, I recognize that this often leads to a beguiling but rather solipsistic Shangri-la, where learning is an individual pleasure rather than a communal one. In attempting to reposition learning as a shared activity, I employ Lorraine Code's (2006) ecological thinking, which demands that knowledge itself and the way it is understood must be reconfigured in terms of mutuality and respect for the interconnectedness of all things. Applying this concept to the learners in my studies, I am able to trace the ways in which they desire knowledge that is communal, responsible and respectful to the needs of others, yet this is consistently blocked within the education system. I conclude by reiterating that an ecological vision of learning and knowledge, which holds together difference and similitude in a harmonious whole, is indeed an idealized picture, but also a vitally necessary one for belonging and survival.

# Conclusion

In this chapter, I will summarize the key conclusions and arguments I am making in the book and particularly focus on the significance of the concept of imagined social capital and its opportunities and limitations. I also want to take some opportunity to reflect on the conditions of its production, as a book written on many an 'Evening train', as evoked in the poem by Denise Levertov (2002): 'we move through our lives, swiftly, steadily, the train rocks'.

While not claiming that the book attains the status of art, the following description has some resonance for me:

> . . . art is not perceived as a simple vehicle for the expression of the solitary subjects contents that the viewer comes along and reads off, dispassionately or affectingly. Instead art may open up a space between subjects, projected and imagined in the making, recalled and projecting in the responding, that can, by mediation of the shared space of the work, cause transformations on both sides, even delayed in time.
>
> (Pollock 2007, p. 258)

Rather than being a point at which I, as writer, transmit to you, as reader, the contents of my thinking as a 'solitary subject', the book is a 'shared space' where possible transformations might take place and the impacts it has, or not, on both of us cannot be anticipated.

## Celebrating imagined social capital

In the first part of this concluding chapter, I want to return to the question of imagined social capital, as it lies at the heart of what I am arguing about learning to belong. I have found imagined social capital a useful and creative concept to work with, and end the book even more convinced that it is the imagined and not the pragmatic that offers a way forward when trying to understand learners' lives and create better opportunities for them. As Bachelard (1994) argues, the imagined faces the future and allows us to slip the bounds of automated behaviour. Without the imagined, we are stuck in the regimes that have become familiar and engrained; those regimes which have generally proved negative ones for the learners in my studies. Making symbolic connections with others they know, or imagining networks with others they can only dream of knowing, helps to create benefits of power and resistance. Imagined social capital provides a counter to those factors and processes which tend to fix them firmly in a negative and deficit place. This is not an argument for sidestepping materiality or ignoring inequalities and structural boundaries, but rather a claim that a strong resource for resisting and opposing inequality lies in the imagined realm. Imagined social capital is a start rather than an end point and there are no guarantees of shifting the bounds of poverty and class, as the book demonstrates. Nevertheless, without imagined social capital there are no grounds on which to build an alternative future. Moreover, the imagined and the material co-produce each other; they are not separate entities, and, as the feminist artist Bobby Baker demonstrates, through the symbolic resonance of the materiality of everyday life, new opportunities for thinking and practice emerge (Heathfield 2007). Following this principle, instead of rationalizing what learners should learn and how it should happen, imposing a polemical or purely theoretical framework on this book, I have chosen instead to explore their embodied accounts of learning and non-learning and how these generate situated forms of imagined social capital. In seeing these accounts as embodied, I am also recognizing them as breaking any bounds of what might be recognized as 'identity'. These unselves are perpetually changing and mutating and my studies reveal that we have not yet created a learning system which mirrors and responds to this state of flux or that fosters imagined social capital.

## Critiquing imagined social capital

I would like here to reflect on how I have generated my own imagined social capital, and, as a corrective to my avowed enthusiasm, to think through the possible dangers of this concept. One of the proxies I have been reading while writing this text is a book about the relationship between Simone de Beauvoir and Jean Paul Sartre (Rowley 2005). Like many other feminists growing up in the 1970s, one of the figures with whom I built imagined connections was Simone de Beauvoir. Her widely circulated life iconography played a key role in summoning this up. Her room with high shelves lined with books, and no kitchen, spoke particularly strongly to me – freeing her up from domesticity to live a self-sufficient life in cafés and bars. The interesting thing here is not how 'special' this identification made me but how generic. Along with countless others I had entered into a set of endlessly regressing mirrors. It appears that de Beauvoir herself created her persona partly through imagined connections with Katherine Mansfield, who had herself developed the cult of 'the solitary woman' in her fiction:

> When I lunched in the Canebiere, upstairs at the Brasserie O' Central, or had dinner at the back of Charley's Tavern – a cool dark place, its walls covered with photographs of boxers – I told myself that I too personified this "solitary woman". I felt the same while I was drinking coffee under the plane trees on the Place de la Prefecture, or sitting by a window of the Café Cintra down at the Old Port.
>
> (Simone de Beauvoir, quoted in Rowley 2005, p. 47)

So, ironically, the solitary woman takes her power from being part of a network of women all performing self-conscious solitariness. Their move is to place themselves, by choice, outside the community of others. In this they like to distinguish themselves from the lonely and exploited woman, such as those found in the pages of Jean Rhys (1939).

As I finish this book in solitary confinement in a small hotel in London, taking breaks to sit in literary cafés, the imagined social capital generated by this imagined network makes the experience possible, and even pleasurable, and transforms loneliness into power.

It is possible to take this example and use it to critique the usefulness of imagined social capital. My network of 'solitary women' could be seen as is generic and second hand. What if the benefits accrued, say here in ways in which women might imagine themselves as powerful and free, are contaminated by ugly facts? Does my reading of Rowley and growing awareness of de Beauvoir's exploitation of young women and dependence on the goodwill of men negate the imagined social capital her persona had accrued? I think not, because the benefit is not attached to her personally, but to what she represents and what uses can be made of that by others. The capital may be spent wisely in mirroring the good of de Beauvoir, her intelligence, hard work and love of life or its might be spent foolishly in copying her selfishness and self-delusions, but in itself it is neutral.

One of the obvious dangers of imagined social capital is that it might be seen as freeing institutions and policy from any obligation to address structural inequalities. This is a serious critique and the answer must be that in addressing inequalities imagined social capital is facilitated: the relationship is a mutual one. As I shall discuss, imagined social capital can be helped or hindered by changes to practice. There is also the point that like other forms of social capital, imagined social capital must be legitimated in order to act as currency. There must be conditions which enable the symbolic power to be operationalized. To return to the Simone de Beauvoir question, her symbolic power worked for women such as myself because it coincided with opportunities in the welfare state, such as grants and funds to support university entry and with cultural shifts of feminism. As I have indicated earlier, by stressing the significance of imagined social capital I by no means wish to ignore materiality.

Why talk in terms of social capital at all when for many it is considered a debased neo-liberal concept? For myself, this challenge to insert the imagined into the strictly rational is one of the most alluring facets of this discussion. To suggest that networks are important, but they may not be what they seem, and that the most 'efficient' are the symbolic, is a pleasing conceit. I do not see the imagined social capital concept as being subsumed by social capital mores, but as subverting and transforming them.

## Counter-imagining imagined social capital

Imagined social capital can also be a means of making unexpected and challenging connections. There are important opportunities to create imagined social capital, not by forging imagined networks with the powerful and privileged, such as de Beauvoir, but by making symbolic connections with the marginalized and those resisting oppression. We could conceptualize this as a process of 'counter-imagining'. In order to create positive imagined social capital in this context, we first have to counter the negative imagining which has placed groups of people in a deficit position. M. Jacqui Alexander throws down a challenge to higher education, and specifically to feminists within the university, as to how they might facilitate a changed relationship with such communities:

> Teaching for justice must interrogate whether feminism has perhaps bought into the script of an unwieldy state in its continued erasure of the political agendas of poor and working class people's struggle. Does this practice travel into our classroom and erase these same histories and the histories of immigrant women from our syllabi? Do our analytic practices turn indispensability into victimhood, thereby reproducing the dominant script that rewrites citizenship in the names of the members of the corporate class only.
>
> (Alexander 2005, p. 114)

According to the women students I researched, their university curriculum did just what Alexander is describing. For example, Katy, a working class mature student, was highly critical of the ethnocentricity in Environmental Studies, where women, where they existed at all, were always imagined as victims:

Katy:  When it's Western it's just men, but when it's the Third World it's just the put-upon woman.

JQ:  What does it leave out?

Katy:  They are not victims, they are running the household.

In order to forge networks with these strong women, and potentially make globalized links with them, at both a material and imagined level, first they must be taken out of the limited categories Western imagination (and Western academic disciplines) have cast them into, by a process of counter-imagination.

The 'indispensable' also become 'victims' closer to home too. In the UK this can be seen in the way that the young people in jobs without training (JWT) are repeatedly swallowed up in the category of NEET – those who are not in education, employment or training, and who need most of all to be disciplined. Software companies advertise packages to local authorities to help them 'manage your NEETS', and prevent this dangerous category of young people from getting out of hand. The conflation of JWT with NEET ignores the very fact that the young people in jobs without training do have jobs, jobs that they often value and that these jobs in cafés, hotels and shops keep towns and cities going and allow the middle classes their leisure. These young people are indeed indispensable and it is very difficult to see how our society could run without them. Yet when recognized at all, they are seen as simply lacking any form of solid citizenship. The roles that they undertake are not allowed to have symbolic value and are simply erased. Part of what I have tried to do here is recoup the symbolic value of these learners' accounts and cut through and counter-imagine the negative images of the dominant script.

## Facilitating imagined social capital

One of the questions I have been asked is how can we create imagined social capital for learners? This is something of a misguided question, as the point of imagined social capital is that it is something learners create for themselves. However, it is legitimate to consider how the production of imagined social capital might be facilitated within a learning environment. One of the clear messages of this book is that establishing cosy learning communities in which difference is smoothed out, and systems of regulation are cloaked in worthy sentiments of community, is not conducive to imagined social capital or belonging. Instead we have to let in and welcome the stranger and most of all acknowledge our own strangeness. New and challenging concepts, new configurations of knowledge help to feed imagined and symbolic connections, opening up possibilities for learners.

> It's all very well offering people a cup of tea when they come through the door but you like to offer them a little bit more, something that's going to stretch them. Give them something to wake their brain up a bit.
>
> (Tom, support worker homeless organization)

However, this will not work unless we acknowledge that the learner is not a blank slate, that they already know interesting and valuable things and the capacity for making symbolic and imagined connections already exists – it is not in the teacher's gift of patronage. A good example here is the body art lecture which so engaged the homeless learners. As Alexander argues, this balance is not an easy process:

> . . . we confront a major difficulty in reconciling desire with practice, of teaching a vision we have not yet fully lived, of moving inside and across the outlines of a map with no guarantees. Such work places a great demand on the imagination.
>
> (ibid., p. 112)

I cannot provide a handbook for imagined social capital – such a thing could not exist – what I do suggest is that in order to facilitate imagined social capital for learners, we first have to take it, and them, seriously.

## Summary of the book

In this book I have taken a winding path through many ideas and issues, deliberately winding, because I do not believe in fixed pathways as an appropriate metaphor for the lives of learners. My source material has been research data from the lives of over 200 learners, all in some ways occupying marginal positions in the educational world. These include women students in higher education, working class students who have dropped out of university in provincial areas of decline, young people in jobs without training in rural areas and people learning in the voluntary sector in homeless organizations and community arts projects in inner cities. To start the journey I identified how I was positioning these learners not as authentic, inescapable or self-made selves, but as 'unselves', never being fixed into anything as tangible as an 'identity'. The difficulties and implications of sustaining this position are discussed, in relation to such key concerns as voice, narrative and emotion. I then move on to analysing the ways in which the field of education has tried to create belonging for learners' 'selves' by means of learning communities and communities of practice. I critique these ideas as being retrogressive and restrictive and posit instead Iris Marion Young's (1990) vision of the 'unoppressive city', where learners are allowed to be different and benign 'strangers', who respect and celebrate each other's difference, and move to discuss how my studies validate such an interpretation. I then argue that learners create belonging and power for themselves, not via the paraphernalia of learning communities, but by the generation of imagined social capital: the benefits they create through symbolic and imagined networks. Imagined social capital is understood as situated and localized, and the different manifestations in my research studies are analysed, drawing in particular on ideas of nature, nostalgia and abjection. The book then moves to consider how 'home', belonging and learning are spatialized. It starts by exploring the different configurations and impacts of house and home in my studies, including the home town. Then it considers how we might respatialize learning so that learning that is ignored and devalued, such as the love of informal learning amongst young, white, working class men, becomes validated. A respatialization of formal learning environments is also proposed, offering new relations between 'smooth' and striated' space and accredited and non-accredited learning. This section of the book concludes with a challenge to the prevailing discourse of 'waste of space' which characterizes the way the learners in my studies are positioned, demonstrating the many ways in which they resist this positioning. Finally, in opposition to the waste of space discourse, the book offers another vision, that of a joy of knowledge which places the learners as part of a unified cosmic belonging. It argues that challenges to the master's knowledge have had less impact than might be hoped upon mainstream constructions of valid knowledge. Moving from what knowledge should be, to an embodied account of how joy of knowledge manifests itself is another way forward. Lorraine Code's (2006) ideas of ecological thinking are used to analyze the kinds of knowledge the learners in my study want. It is revealed that, rather than the competitive, hierarchical and joyless model offered to them, they want relational, communal and mutual forms of knowledge that might be used to make the world more pleasurable and socially just. Rather than promoting belonging in a tight learning community we need a cosmic belonging recognizing the unity and interdependence of all things.

## Coda: Taking the train

The following quotation from de Certeau seems to summon up the relationship between the train passenger and the world outside, a regal but rather ridiculous sense of moving while everything else stands still. It was highly evocative to read it on a train across Yorkshire, while writing this book, as it captures both the hope and the pretension of trying to remove oneself from the world in order to create 'unknown landscapes':

> Outside there is another immobility, that of things, towering mountains, stretches of green field and forest, arrested villages, colonades of buildings, black urban silhouettes against the pink evening sky, the twinkling of nocturnal lights on a sea that precedes or succeeds our histories . . . a speculative experience of the world: being outside of these things that

stay there . . . Glass and iron produce speculative thinkers or Gnostics, this cutting-off is necessary for the birth, outside of these things but not without them, of unknown landscapes and the strange fables of our private lives . . . Everyone goes back to work . . . Hand-to-hand combat begins again with a reality that dislodges the spectator without rails or windowpanes. There comes to an end the Robinson Crusoe adventure of the travelling noble soul that could believe itself *intact* because it was surrounded by glass and iron.

(de Certeau 1984, pp. 111–14, original emphasis)

For me this extract is both chastening and hilarious as it shows me to myself as if reflected in the train window:

*Laugh out loud on the train reading de Certeau and his description of train journeys. Think about what it means for the production of this book and other texts. The parody of melancholy and the Robinson Crusoe 'noble soul' make sense to me as does the hand to hand combat – Does writing also become a means of seeing the thing you are separated from and luxuriating in that separation? The bringing close is actually the pushing away?*

(J. Q., research diary)

Thinking about the production of the text and how much of it has been borne along in train journeys across England: in the end the journeys bring me no closer to knowing either myself or others, including the participants of this book, but that is OK. The seeker is always unsure and asks themselves questions every day about the meanings of their actions. This is the spirit in which this book is offered; in conscious resistance to those who are always certain they know best. For 'the hegemony of certainty leaves us with its pitiful products: zero tolerance, fear of failure and technocratic language . . . Let us return research to what it does not know, to let that ignorance come out' (Britzman 2006, p. ix). 'Know-ability' implies a kind of completion, and the ethos of this book is that the incomplete and the imagined, the moving and the uncentred all bring us closer to learning and to belonging. They are to be welcomed and celebrated.

# Bibliography

Ahmed, S. (2000), *Strange Encounters: Embodied Others in Post-Coloniality*. London: Routledge.

— (2004), *The Cultural Politics of Emotion*. Edinburgh: Edinburgh University Press.

Alexander, M. J. (2005), *Pedagogies of Crossing: Meditations on Feminism, Sexual Politics, Memory and the Sacred*. Durham, NC: Duke University Press.

Archer, L., Hollingworth, S. and Mendick, H. (2010, forthcoming), *Urban Youth and Education*. Buckingham: Open University Press.

Archer, L., Hutchings, M. and Ross, A. (2003), *Higher Education and Social Class*. London: Routledge.

Bachelard, G. (1994 edn), *The Poetics of Space*. Boston, MA: Beacon Press.

Ball, S. J., Maguire, M. and Macrae, S. (1999), 'Young lives, diverse choices and imagined futures in an education and training market'. *International Journal of Inclusive Education*, 3 (3), 195–224.

Beck, U. and Beck-Gernsheim, E. (2002), *Individualization*. London: Sage.

Bhabha, H. K. (2005), 'Are you a man or a mouse?', in M. Berger, B. Wallis and S. Watson (eds), *Constructing Masculinity*. London: Routledge.

Biesta, G. (2009), 'What kind of theory for Higher Education'. Invited paper, Society for Research in Higher Education seminar, *The Place of Theory in Higher Education Scholarship*. London Metropolitan University, 29 January.

Bishop E. (1991), *Complete Poems*. London: Chatto and Windus.

Blaxter, L. and Hughes, C. (2000), 'Social capital: a critique', in J. Thompson (ed.), *Stretching the Academy*. Leicester: NIACE, pp. 80–94.

Bourdieu, P. (1997), 'The forms of capital', in A. H. Halsey, H. Laudner, P. Brown and A. S. Wells (eds), *Education, Culture, Economy, Society*. Oxford: Oxford University Press, pp. 46–58.

Bowles, G. and Duelli-Klein, R. (eds) (1983), *Theories of Women's Studies*, London: Routledge and Kegan Paul.

Braidotti, R. (1994), *Nomadic Subjects: Embodiment and Sexual Difference in Contemporary Feminist Theory*. New York: Columbia University Press.

Barnett, R. (1997), *Higher Education: A Critical Business*. Buckingham: SRHE and Open University Press.

Barnett, R. (2003), *Beyond All Reason*. Buckingham: SRHE and Open University Press.

Britzman, B. (2006), *Novel Education*. New York: Peter Lang.

Burke, P. J. and Jackson, S. (2007), *Reconceptualising Lifelong Learning: Feminist Interventions*. London: Routledge.

Burman, E. (2008), 'Beyond "emotional literacy" in feminist and educational research', *British Educational Research Journal*, 35, 137–55.

Cassen, R. and Kingdon, G. (2007), *Low Educational Achievement*. York, Joseph Rowntree Foundation.

Christie, H. (2009), 'Emotional journeys: young people and transitions to university', *British Journal of Sociology of Education*, 30 (2), 123–37.

Code, L. (1991), *What Can She Know?: Feminist Theory and the Construction of Knowledge*. Ithaca, NY: Cornell University Press.

— (2006), *Ecological Thinking: The Politics of Epistemic Location*. Oxford: Oxford University Press.

Coleman, J. S. (1990), *Foundations of Social Theory*. London: Harvard Press.

Coleridge, S. T. (1975 edn), *Biographia Literaria*. London: Dent.

Colley, H. (2007), 'Understanding time in learning transitions through the lifecourse', *International Studies in Sociology of Education*, 17 (4), 427–43.

Colley, H., Hodkinson, P. and Malcolm, J. (2003), *Informality and Formality in Learning*. London: Learning and Skills Research Centre.

Dasgupta, P. (2002), 'Social capital and economic performance: analytics working paper', Cambridge: Faculty of Economics and Politics: University of Cambridge. Available at: www.econ.cam.ac.uk/faculty/dasgupta (accessed 11 January 2010).

Davies, S. Lubelska, C. and Quinn, J. (1994), *Changing the Subject: Women in Higher Education*. London: Taylor and Francis.

de Certeau, M. (1984), *The Practice of Everyday Life*. London: University of California Press.

de Lauretis, T. (1987), *Technologies of Gender*. London: MacMillan.

Deleuze, G. and Guattari, F. (1980), *A Thousand Plateau*. Minneapolis: University of Minnesota Press.

Department for Children, Schools and Families (DCSF) (2008), *Reducing the Number of Young People not in Education, Employment or Training (NEET): The Strategy*. London: The Stationary Office.

Department for Education and Skills (DfES) (2003a), *The Future of Higher Education*. London: Stationery Office.

— (2003b), *Widening Participation in Higher Education*. London: Stationery Office.

— (2003c) 'We can crack "lad culture" – Miliband', press notice. Available online at www.dfes.gov.uk (accessed 19 July 2005).

Department for Innovation, Universities and Skills (DIUS) (2008), *Higher Education and Work, High Skills: High Value*. London: The Stationery Office.

— (2008a), *Informal Adult Learning – Shaping the Way Ahead*. University and Skills' Consultation, January, London: The Stationery Office.

— (2008b), *Informal Adult Learning – Shaping the Way Ahead, Consultation Response Analysis Report*, October, London: The Stationery Office.

Diski, J. (2006), *On Trying to Keep Still*. London: Virago.

Doucet, A. and Mauthner, N. (2008), 'What can be known and how? Narrated subjects and the Listening Guide'. *Qualitative Research*, 8 (3), 399–409.

Duffy, C. A. (1990), *The Other Country*. London: Anvil Press.

Ecclestone, K. (2004), personal communication.

Ecclestone, K. Blackmore, T., Biesta, G., Colley, H. and Hughes, M. (2005), 'Transitions through the lifecourse: political, professional and academic perspectives', paper presented at Annual TLRP/ESRC Conference, Warwick University.

Ecclestone, K. and Hayes, D. (2008), *The Dangerous Rise of Therapeutic Education*. London: Routledge.

Edwards, R., Biesta, G. and Thorpe, M. (2009), *Rethinking Contexts for Learning and Teaching*, London: Routledge.

Ellsworth, E. (1989), 'Why doesn't this feel empowering? Working through repressive myths of critical pedagogy'. *Harvard Educational Review*, 59 (3), 297–334.

Field, J. (2003), 'Civic engagement and lifelong learning: survey findings on social capital and attitudes towards learning', *Studies in the Education of Adults*, 35 (2), 142–56.

— (2005), *Social Capital and Lifelong Learning*. Bristol: Policy Press.

Foucault, M. (1980), 'Two lectures', in C. Gordon (ed.) *Power/Knowledge: Selected Interviews and Other Writings, 1972–1977*. Brighton: Harvester Press.

Frame, J. (2008), *Storms Will Tell: Selected Poems*. Highgreen: Bloodaxe Books.

Francis, B. and Skelton, C. (2005), *Reassessing Gender and Achievement*. London: Routledge.

— (2008), '"The self-made self": analysing the potential contribution to gender and education of theories that disembed selfhood'. *Discourse*, 29 (3), 311–25.

Furedi, F. (2009) *Wasted: Why Education isn't Educating*. London: Continuum.

Fuller, A. and Biesta, G. (2008), 'Learning through the lifecourse'. Presentation at Teaching Learning Research Programme conference, 'Improving Teaching: Enhancing Learning. Connecting Evidence, Practice and Policy'. London, 25 October.

Gaitskill, M. (2008), *Veronica*. London: Serpent's Tail.

Gereluk, D. (2006), *Education and Community*. London: Continuum.

Giddens, A. (1991), *Modernity and Self-Identity: Self and Society in the Late Modern Age*. Cambridge: Polity Press.

Ginsberg, A. (2006), *Collected Poems 1947–1997*. New York: HarperCollins.

Golding, B, Harvey, J. and Echter, A. (2004), *Men's Learning Through ACE and Community Involvement in Small Rural Towns*. Report to Adult Community and FE Board, Victoria [Australia].

Grinberg, S. (2009), 'Regulation, resistance and activism: troubling margin and centre'. Plenary panel, Gender and Education Association conference, London, 25–27 March.

Grosz, E. (1994), *Volatile Bodies: Towards a Corporeal Feminism*. Bloomington, IN: Indiana University Press.

Haylett, C. (2001), 'Illegitimate Subjects? Abject whites, neo-liberal modernisation and middle class multiculturalism'. *Environment and Planning D: Society and Space*, 19 (3), 351–70.

Heathfield, A. (2007) 'Risk in Intimacy: An Interview with Bobby Baker', in M. Barrett and B. Baker (eds), *Bobby Baker: Redeeming Features of Everyday Life*, London: Routledge.

Hey, V. (2003), 'Joining the club? Academia and working class femininities'. *Gender and Education*, 15 (3), 319–35.

Hirsch, M. and Smith, V. (2002), 'Feminism and cultural memory: an introduction'. *Signs*, 28 (1), 1–19.

Hollingworth, S. Beedell, P. Jamieson, F. and Williams, K. (2007), '"It's down to the individual": pupil's discourses about social and educational inequalities'. British Education Research Association Annual Conference. Institute of Education, University of London. 5–8 September.

Hooks, B. (1994), *Teaching to Transgress*. London: Routledge.

Hustvedt, S. (2006), *A Plea for Eros*. London: Hodder and Stoughton Limited.

Jackson, C. (2006), *Lads and Ladettes in School*. Maidenhead: Open University Press.

Kristeva, J. (1982), *Powers of Horror: An Essay on Abjection*. New York: Columbia.

Lapping, C. (2009), 'Passionate attachments in disciplinary practices'. Symposium, Gender and Education conference, Institute for Education, London, 25–27 March.

Lave, J. and Wenger, E. (1991), *Situated Learning: Legitimate Peripheral Participation*. Cambridge: Cambridge University Press.

Lawy, R. (2002), 'Transformation of person, identity and understanding: a case study'. *British Journal of Sociology of Education*, 24 (3), 331–45.

— (2006), 'Connective learning: young people's identity and knowledge-making in work and non-work contexts'. *British Journal of Sociology of Education*, 27 (3), 325–40.

Learning and Skills Council (2003), *Successful Participation for All*. Coventry: Learning and Skills Council.

Leathwood, C. and Hey, V. (2009), 'Gender/ed discourses and emotional sub-texts: theorising emotion in higher education. *Teaching in Higher Education*, 14 (4), 429–40.

Leigh-Smith, B., MacGregor, J., Matthews, R. S., and Gabelnik, F. (2004), *Learning Communities: Reforming Undergraduate Education*. New York: Jossey-Bass.

Leitch, S. (2006), *Leitch Review of Skills Prosperity for All in the Global Economy – World Class Skills*. London: HMSO.

Levertov, D. (2002), *Evening Train Selected Poems*. New York: New Directions Books.

Lorde, A. (1984), *Sister Outsider*, Trumansburg, New York: The Crossing Press.

Martin, J. R. (1994), *Changing the Educational Landscape: Philosophy, Women and Curriculum*. London: Routledge.

Martino, W. (1999), '"Cool boys", "party animals", "squids" and "poofters": interrogating the dynamics and politics of adolescent masculinities in school'. *British Journal of Sociology of Education*, 20 (2), 239–63.

Mayo, M. (2000), 'Learning for active citizenship: training for and learning from participation in area regeneration'. *Studies in the Education of Adults*, 32 (1), 22–35.

McCarthy, C. (2009), 'Keynote speech'. Discourse, Power and Resistance conference, Manchester, 6–8 April.

McDowell, L. (2007), 'Respect, respectability, deference and place: what is the problem with/for working class boys?' *Geoforum*, 38 (2), 276–86.

McGivney, V. (1999), *Informal Learning in the Community*. Leicester: NIACE.

— (2004), *Men Earn Women Learn*. Leicester: NIACE.

McKay A. (2000), *Giving Shine*. County Donegal: Summer Palace Press.

Mellor, L. (2007), *Natural Attraction and Convivial Conversation*. Times Higher Education, 14th September, pp. 18–19.

Merrill. B. and West, L. (2009), *Using Biographical Methods in Social Research*. London: Sage.

Milburn, A. (2009), *Unleashing Aspirations: The Final Report of the Panel on Fair Access to the Professions*. London: Cabinet Office.

Minh-ha, T. T. (1990), 'Cotton and iron', in R. Ferguson, M. Gever and T. T. Minh-ha (eds), *Out There: Marginalization and Contemporary Cultures*. New York and Cambridge, MA: New Museum of Contemporary Art and Massachusetts Institute of Technology.

Moore, L. (2009), *The Collected Stories*. London: Faber and Faber.

Mynott, J. (2009), *Birdscapes: Birds in Our Imagination and Experience*. New York: Princeton Press.

National Audit Office (NAO) (2008), *Widening Participation in Higher Education*, London: Stationery Office.

National Institute for Adult and Community Education (NIACE) (2008), Response to the DIUS consultation on *Adult Informal Learning – Shaping the Way Ahead*. Leicester: NIACE.

Nayak, A. (2006), 'Displaced masculinities: chavs, youth and class in the post-industrial city'. *Sociology*, 40 (5), 813–31.

Noyes, A. (2004), 'Learning landscapes'. *British Educational Research Journal*, 30 (1), 27–43.

Ollin, R. (2002), 'Knowledge is a team pursuit'. Times Higher Education Supplement, 7 June, p. 16.

Oswald, A. (2002), *Dart*. London: Faber and Faber.

Pile, S. and Thrift, N. (1995) *Mapping the Subject: Geographies of Cultural Transformation*. London: Routledge.

Pile, S. and Thrift, N. (eds) (2000), *City A–Z: Urban Fragments*. London: Routledge.

Plummer, K. (1995), *Telling Sexual Stories*. New York: Routledge.

Pollock, G. (2007), 'Diary drawings', in M. Barrett and B. Baker (eds), *Bobby Baker: Redeeming Features of Daily Life*. London: Routledge.

Popkewitz, T. E. (2007), *Cosmopolitanism and the Age of School Reform*. New York: Routledge.

Probyn, E. (1996), *Outside Belongings*. London: Routledge.

Puttnam, R. D. (2000), *Bowling Alone: The Collapse and Revival of American Community*. New York: Simon Schuster.

Quinn, J. (2003a), *Powerful Subjects: Are Women Really Taking Over the University*. Stoke on Trent: Trentham Books.

— (2003b), 'The dynamics of the protected space: spatial concepts and women students'. *British Journal of the Sociology of Education*, 24 (4), 449–63.

— (2004a), 'Understanding working class "drop out" from higher education through a socio-cultural lens: cultural narratives and local contexts'. *International Studies in Sociology of Education*, 14 (1), 57–75.

— (2004b), 'Mothers, learners and countermemory'. *Gender and Education*, 16 (3), 365–78.

— (2004c), 'The corporeality of learning', in S. Ali, S. Benjamin and M. Mauthner (eds), *The Politics of Gender and Education*. London: Palgrave.

— (2005a), 'Belonging in a learning community: the re-imagined university and imagined social capital'. *Studies in the Education of Adults*, April.

— (2005b), 'Subjects and subjectivities in higher education'. Paper presented at American Educational Research Associationa (AERA) conference. Montreal, 11–15 April.

— (2006), 'Mass participation but no curriculum transformation', in D. Jary and R. Jones (eds), *The Policy and Practice of Widening Participation in the Social Sciences*. CSAP: University of Birmingham.

Quinn, J., Lawy, R., Diment, K. (2008), *Young People in Job Without Training in South West England: Not Just "Dead-End Kids in Dead-End Jobs"*. Exeter: Marchmont Observatory/Exeter University.

Quinn, J., Thomas, L., Slack, K., Casey, L., Thexton, W. and Noble, J. (2005), *From Life Crisis to Lifelong Learning: Rethinking Working Class 'Drop Out' from Higher Education*. York: York Publishing/Joseph Rowntree Foundation.

— (2006), 'Lifting the hood: lifelong learning and young, white, provincial working-class masculinities'. *British Educational Research Journal*, 32 (5), 735–50.

Quinn, J., Thomas, L., Slack, K., Vigurs, K. and Flynn, N. (2004), 'Learners on their own terms? Learning brokerage, mainstream transformation and social exclusion'. *Journal of Access Policy and Practice*, 3 (1), 21–44.

Reay, D. (1997) Feminist Theory, Habitus and Social Class: disrupting notions of classlessness. *Women's Studies International Forum*, 20, 225–33.

— (2001), 'Finding or losing yourself? Working class relationships to education'. *Journal of Education Policy*, 16 (4), 333–46.

— (2004), '"Mostly roughs and toughs": Social class, race and representation in inner city schooling'. *Sociology*, 35 (4), 1005–23.

— (2006), 'The zombie stalking English schools: social class and educational inequality'. *British Journal of Educational Studies*, 54 (3), 288–307.

Reay, D. and Ball, S. (1997), 'Spoilt for choice: the working classes and educational markets'. *Oxford Review of Education*, 23 (1), 89–101.

Reay, D., Hollingworth, S., Williams, K., Crozier, G., Jamieson, F., James, D. and Beedell, P. (2007), 'A darker shade of pale? Whiteness, the middle classes and multi-ethnic inner city schooling'. *Sociology*, 41 (6), 1041–60.

Rhys, J. (1939), *Good Morning Midnight*. London: Constable.

Ribbens, J. (1994), *Mothers and their Children: A Feminist Sociology of Childrearing*. London: Sage.

Ribbens-McCarthy, J., Edwards, R. and Gillies, V. (2002), *Making Families: Moral Tales of Parenting and Step-parenting*. York: Sociology Press.

Robson, J., Bailey, B. and Mendick, H. (2008), 'Learners' emotional and psychic responses to encounters with learning support in further education and training'. *British Journal of Education Studies*, 56 (3), 304–23.

Rose, G. (1993), *Feminism and Geography*. Cambridge: Polity.

Rose, N. (2002), *The Intellectual Life of the British Working Classes*. Reading: Yale University Press.

Rowley, H. (2005), *Tête á-Tête: Simone de Beauvoir and Jean-Paul Sartre*. New York: Harper-Collins.

Royle, M. (2003), *The Uncanny*. Manchester: Manchester University Press.

Savin-Baden, M. (2008), *Learning Spaces: Creating Opportunities for Knowledge Creation in Academic Life*. Maidenhead: SRHE/Open University Press.

St Pierre, E. (1997), 'Nomadic enquiry in the smooth spaces of the field: a preface'. *International Journal of Qualitative Studies in Education*, 10 (3), 365–85.

Schostack, J. and Schostack, J. (2006), 'Radical methodologies: social justice, judgement, knowledge and education'. Paper presented at British Educational Research Association (BERA) conference, University of Warwick, 6–9 September.

Skeggs, B. (1997), *Formations of Class and Gender*. London: Sage.

Smith, D. E. (1999), 'Keynote speech'. Autobiography seminar series, Institute for Women's Studies, University of Lancaster.

Social Justice Policy Group (2007), 'Ending the Costs of Social Breakdown', Vol 3: Educational Failure, *Breakthrough Britain*.

Tarleton, A. (2003), 'Wrong course, wrong time'. *Guardian Unlimited*, 7 March.

Tamboukou, M. (2008), 'Machinic assemblages: women, art education and space'. *Discourse: Studies in the Cultural Politics of Education*, 29 (3), 359–75.

Tedder, M. and Biesta, G. J. J. (2009), 'Biography, transition and learning in the lifecourse', in J. Field, J. Gallacher and R. Ingram (eds) (2009), *Researching Transitions in Lifelong Learning*. London: Routledge, pp. 76–90.

Thomas, G. (2007) *Education and Theory: Strangers in Paradigms*. Abingdon: Open University Press.

Thomas, L. and Quinn, J. (2007) *First Generation Entry into Higher Education: An International Study*. Buckingham: SRHE: Open University Press.

Thomas, L., Quinn, J., Slack, K., Casey, L., Vigurs, K. and Flynn, N. (2004), *Learning Brokers Research Project: Report 1*. London: Learning and Skills Research Centre.

Tinto, V. (1997), 'Classrooms as communities: exploring the educational character of student persistence'. *Journal of Higher Education*, 68 (6), 599–623.

Tinto, V. (2003), 'Establishing conditions for student success', in L. Thomas, M. Cooper and J. Quinn (eds) (2003), *Improving Completion Rates amongst Disadvantaged Students*. Stoke on Trent: Trentham Books, pp. 1–11.

Tonkiss, F. (2000), 'A–Z', in S. Pile and N. Thrift (eds), *City A–Z: Urban Fragments*. London: Routledge, pp. 1–3.

Waters, S. (2009), *The Little Stranger*. London: Virago.

Watts, M. and Bridges, D. (2006), 'The value of non-participation in higher education'. *Journal of Education Policy*, 21 (3), 267–89.

Webb, S. and Warren, S. (2009), 'Who is the "responsible learner"? Viewing learning careers through social narratives and recursive methodology', in J. Field, J. Gallacher and R. Ingram (eds) (2009), *Researching Transitions in Lifelong Learning*. London: Routledge, pp. 50–65.

Wenger, E. (1998), *Communities of Practice: Learning, Meaning and Identity*. Cambridge: Cambridge University Press.

Whaley, P. (2000), 'Missionary and other positions: the community, the university and widening participation', in J. Thompson (ed.), *Stretching the Academy*. Leicester: NIACE.

Whitman, W. (1964), *Leaves of Grass*. London: Everyman.

Woolcock, M. (1998) 'Social capital and economic development: towards a theoretical synthesis and policy framework'. *Theory and Society*, 27, 151–208.

Woolf, V. (1979), *Women and Writing*. London: Women's Press.

Wray, M. and Newitz, A. (1997), *White Trash: Race and Class in America*. London: Routledge.

Young, I. M. (1990), 'The ideal of community and the politics of difference', in L. J. Nicholson, (ed.), *Feminism/Postmodernism*. London: Routledge, pp. 300–23.

Zembylas, M. and Fendler, L. (2007), 'Reframing emotion in education though lenses of *parrhesia* and *care of the self.*, *Studies in Philosophy and Education*, 26 (4), 319–33.

Žižek, S. (1991), *Looking Awry: An Introduction to Jacques Lacan through Popular Culture*. Cambridge, MA and London: MIT Press.

— (2009), 'In 1968, structures walked the street – will they do it again?' in J. Satterthwaite, H. Piper and P. Sikes (eds), *Power in the Academy*. Stoke on Trent: Trentham Books.

# Index

Printed in Great Britain
by Amazon